M000188097

One Shared

Heart

April Waverly

BRIGHTON PUBLISHING LLC
435 N. HARRIS DRIVE
MESA, AZ 85203

ONE SHARED HEART

APRIL WAVERLY

BRIGHTON PUBLISHING LLC
435 N. HARRIS DRIVE
MESA, AZ 85203

WWW.BRIGHTONPUBLISHING.COM

ISBN: 978-1-62183-574-5

PRINTED IN THE UNITED STATES OF AMERICA

First Edition

COVER DESIGN: TOM RODRIGUEZ

Dedication

My Mom inspired this story. Not just because of bagels, but through her deep love for her kids and family. When she found out she was becoming a grandma, she was not only excited for the grandchild she would get to enjoy. She was excited for me to experience this special bond between a mother and her child. Now I can truly appreciate how her love and our bond has shaped who I am today. I will always strive to recreate the world she made for me, for my daughter.

This book is dedicated to my Mom who is my inspiration and my daughter who continues to be my muse.

Foreword

When a fetus is developing, the first organ to form is the heart. The heart takes shape and starts to truly beat at around four weeks. This means that for the first few weeks, you and your mother shared one heart.

Chapter One

PLAYING IN HER ROOM

"No, it's still playtime!" I screamed at my dad while holding my stuffed fish toy in one hand and a DVD box in the other.

"You can still play in there, I can get your new book," he suggested. I scoffed at him without weighing the offer.

I didn't like it in there, it always had a weird smell and I wasn't allowed to do anything. But just like every day it was that time for me to go in the room and see my mom. I was with my mom but at most she just sat smiling at me asking me what I was drawing or what I did that morning. She could never come sit with me and sometimes she would fall asleep. When she would fall asleep I would get close to her bed to touch her or play with her hair if it reached the edge of the bed. When I was close enough I would watch her one item of jewelry reflect back the dull yellow hue of the room.

But, if she was awake or my dad was watching I was never allowed within a few steps of the bed. If I step too close I was ushered away or reminded of how expensive the equipment was. It was no fun at all to be pushed into this dim room with the wide radius around my mom and limited forms of entertainment.

This isn't how it always was. I remember just a few years ago playing outside, going to the beach, and baking with her. I used to be allowed to jump all over her in bed, run around, and chase her in the kitchen while we waited for the pancakes to bubble and steam. Then all of a sudden something changed. First she was away for a really long time, no one really told me why. Then all my toys and furniture in the playroom were moved out into my room and the living room. One morning I woke up and what was the playroom was now filled with a tall bed with beeping screens on both sides. That morning a bunch of strangers brought my mom in on a wheelchair then carried her into the bed. I tried to go in and see her but my dad kept me out of the room for days telling me mom didn't feel well.

One day I heard them both fighting in the room until my dad stormed out looking for me. I was sitting in the living room right outside her door playing with a hair salon doll when he stepped up to the base of the salon stand. "Ready for a bath?" he asked and he crossed the room and entered the bathroom. I heard the bath water start while I sat in confusion. Bath time was after dinner and playtime, not in the middle of the day. I sat there waiting for an explanation, before giving up and returning to my salon. Without warning, my dad came out of the bathroom holding my towel.

"Ready for a bath?" he repeated holding the towel toward me even though I was clear across the room. His face was gloomy and he didn't meet my eyes. I started to question the time and he just stood there frozen in the position waiting for me to enter the bathroom. I rose from my salon taking my time to get to my feet and I walked to the bathroom staring at him. He continued to focus on the floor. I passed by him into the bathroom he let out a long loud breath before lowering to help me undress and hop in.

2

From then on I would get interrupted once a day, bathed and then I would get to play with my mom for a while until she either got too tired or I got too loud. Now I luckily don't have to take a bath every time, I just have to wash my hands with this gross orange soap in my bathroom before I go in her room. The tradition of my daily interruption, hands washing, and quiet play was no longer fun anymore. The soap stung my hands and any small cut would burn like my hand was on fire. No matter how I complained my dad would supervise me washing my hands and urge me to keep scrubbing while I winced in pain. After washing my hands sometimes my dad would take my temperature or make me change if I was outside at all that morning. It was this long process just to be closed in a room; I never understood what the big deal was. Finally, after his approval I would be walked to the room and my dad would take one last look to ensure he approved of my current state before turning the knob with care and opening the room.

I waited patiently and he opened the door. The thing was I still loved seeing my mom; I just wish it was like before and we could go outside, bake, or play a real game with her. Not just be near her.

I was limited to what I could bring in the room and what I could do while in there. Loud noises were not allowed and I couldn't practice my gymnastics or even move too fast. There were so many rules and every now and then a new one would be added. I used to bring my toys in there until I brought my favorite fish to a sleepover and my dad found out, since then Fishie and any other stuffed animal is not allowed past the doorway. Shoes too, unless they were brand new. I would have to be barefoot or in clean socks. So it was hard playing with mom.

Today I wasn't ready for the interruption; I was just starting the movie he told me I could watch since it was a Saturday. I collected the DVD from the shelf and was excited to reenact the movie with Fishie and his friends that all laid out on the floor in front of the TV where I threw them just a moment ago. I heard it coming this time too. Usually, my mom will talk in a whisper to my dad before he comes out to summon me. I pretended not to hear while he approached and hoped my suspicions were wrong. He interrupted my walk to the television and I felt myself grow angry.

"I want to play out here!" I screamed back stomping toward the TV while watching his reflection in the glass. I watched it get bigger until I turned and he was kneeling behind me.

"I know you don't always like it in there, but your mom loves seeing you and she's feeling better today" he paused pointing to the closed door, "If you would just go in, please Emma."

I kept my face in a tight grimace and squeezed the small soft fish under my armpit tighter.

"Come on I'll get you a new coloring book and we can watch your movie later together."

There was always some kind of promise to coerce me to spend some time in her room, usually it involved a new coloring book or crayons. I prefer to make my own drawings, but my mom always kept those in her room and would ask for more of my creations. I like to show off my drawings to dad, grandpa, and my friends. But whatever I draw in her room doesn't make it to my personal collection or the clips on the fridge. My mom just looks at them and then gets rid of them all. I never get to see these creations again. So sometimes I won't even tell her about the ones I make when I'm not in her room, that way I can hang them on my wall in my room. I have a whole wall of art and show grandpa each time he comes.

I stood there feeling my anger wash around in my stomach and continued to grimace showing I wouldn't give in. He always looked sad and worried while we went back and forth with our ritualistic argument before I would be escorted to my mom's room for playtime. I watched him study me then broke eye contact and looked down at the floor between us. When my eyes met his again he had moved on to his humble and hurt expression. His eyes were always on the brink of tears when it came to my mom. I gave in yet again looking to the closed door my mom lay behind. I did want to see her. I wanted to see her every time we did this dance, but just not in that room.

I let my gaze break from my waiting father, I looked behind him to the pale wood door that separated us from my mom. The door looked eerie and dark since the light in this room was lighter than the open living room it shared a wall with. The door was bruised in several places from the equipment that had to squeeze through the small opening when they were brought home with my mom. The space in the wall had faint beeping and air noises all the time, so I almost always had some movie or song playing to drown out the repetitive dings and whirring.

My eyes faded from my examination of the door, I saw my squinted eyes smiling back at me. Hung just to the right of the door was a silver frame containing one large photo of my mother and me. I was still a baby in the photo and mostly hidden under an over-sized white summer hat. But beaming next to my chubby arm was my mother's face. The photo was taken well before she was sick so she still had a bright smile, full cheeks, gorgeous flowing hair, and these eyes that pulled you in. Her eyes used to be hypnotic; you had to join in her happiness when you met her smiling eyes. I stared at this

5

glossy photo of my mother and me. I felt the tug I always had. I wanted to walk in her room and be reunited with this person. I was always hopeful that one day I would. So I had to go in, just in case.

I dropped the DVD in a sign of defeat, folded my arms and walked to my bathroom to start washing up. Yet another reason I hated this time of the day, I could feel the soap in the familiar cracks of my hands where it always stung. Across the top of my knuckles, the skin was always red and small jagged lines cut through my skin. The soap assaulted these fine lines. I would cry out but my dad would always explain we had to wash up so Mommy wouldn't get any sicker. Either way, I had no option. He would hold my hands under the warm water and scrub while I groaned. After we dried my hands and tidied up my outfit, he walked me into my mom's room.

No one ever told me why but she's always in that room now, some lady comes every morning and evening but she doesn't say much to me. Whenever I see her she just asks me what I'm playing or who I'm dressed as today then makes a weird sad face and goes back into the room. My dad and grandpa are in and out of the room throughout the day, they go in with trays of food and drinks, bowls of water, or bags with those orange pill bottles. My dad reminds me constantly that these bottles are not toys. At some point, I thought one was a musical instrument. He ran at me to rip the bottle from my hands before scurrying back to her room to hide the bottle, he reminded me of this whenever I came within arm's reach of the table that houses the bottles. The door is closed the whole day and everyone that goes in must be clean and healthy so they don't get my mom sick. She is sick already so I am not sure why that matters. I've asked a few times but I get a lot of short answers. The lady tells me to talk to my dad, my grandpa usually tells me mom is sick and we all have to do our part to take care of her so she gets better. My dad alternates between acting like he didn't hear my questions or tells me "It's complicated, you wouldn't understand." And when I ask my mom she usually just tells me that she is fine but just tired.

All I know is my mom is in that room and on that bed and she must stay in that room and on that bed until she is better, whenever that is. Until then, mommy time is after I am clean, when I am healthy, and only in that room.

Since I'm limited to the floor by myself all I can do is talk about my day or color with the beeping and pumping air noise in the background. Sometimes the noise is so loud that my mother will nod her head but I know she can't hear me all the way up on the bed over the noise. Just about the whole room is off-limits. I can't touch any of the beeping screens on the sides of the bed, I can't touch the dresser with any of the pill bottles that sits across from the bed, I can't open the window, I'm not allowed anywhere near her bed, I can't do anything. Thanks to a clumsy moment with the table that usually has some water and food for my mom; I've also been cut off from helping bring anything into the room for her.

I wanted to help my dad one day just carry the cup of water she asked for while I was in there, I stretched my arm up to put the cup on the table and the whole thing dumped on my face and splashed onto the floor. My dad scooped me up and replaced me on the floor by the doorway, the second my feet hit the floor he spun around and crouched on the floor where the water was spilled. He started pushing wires away and drying the area, I apologized but he just kept repeating "Never again, never again". My mom was looking down at him with a scratchy dull voice she was whispering "She didn't mean to, don't panic, I'm sure everything is fine." He continued to dry the floor and the wires while I watched through my wet eyes tears pouring down my cheeks.

One more thing I wasn't allowed to do, I thought. I looked down at my soaked shirt and then at my mom who was talking to me but I couldn't hear anything she was saying. I just started to cry standing there, my mom continued to talk to me with more urgency but I couldn't hear her over my sobs. I escaped the whole situation and just ran from the doorway and plopped on the floor under my clothes in the closet. This was my hiding spot for tears; I wiped my nose and eyes on my hanging clothes and sat there until I was all cried out.

That was the first and last time I tried to help my mom in there and it hung in my memory every time my mom asked for a glass of water. I thought of it again while my dad held a glass in his hands and walked with me to her room today.

I stood in the hallway with my dad and he ran through the 'rules' again before we went in. I know he just did this to get me bored so I wouldn't come in all excited and make too much noise or run around. Today I was already solemn enough thinking of the day with the glass of water, but he did this anyway to ensure I was calm. This is the room of whispers and slow movements. On a typical day, he watches from the doorway until I can prove myself to behave before he leaves me and my mom for our time together.

This tradition of the warnings before creaking the door open was another check he added to my entry to the room. One time, I was still so amped from the morning I jumped on the bed and my dad ripped me away and abruptly dropped me outside the room, then slammed the door. When he opened the door after a long time, I was just standing there apologizing. I didn't know what I did but I knew to never go on that bed again. From that point on it was always the same warnings in the same order. He stared down at me and I waited behind the closed door with him. I learned that the more still I stayed and the less eager I looked the faster his speech would go. He closed as he always did "Now you promise you're going to be careful in there, right?" I nodded and continued to stare at the closed door. He touched my forehead which looked like he was verifying my thoughts but I know he was double-checking to be sure I had no fever.

Chapter Two

The Last Time

*I*n *we go, again, to that room* I thought. He turned the knob to her room. My dad opened the door to the usual dull light filled the space then that weird smell assaulted my nose. I looked and my mom was sitting almost upright on the bed telling me I was her beautiful little girl and asking what I wanted to draw today.

I looked up at her, my mom looked lighter each day. More like a ghost than a person. When she first came home she had skin like mine, but now her skin was closer to the color of her sheets than my skin tone. She used to have hair that covered her shoulders and would hide her pillows at times making it look as if she were sitting on a small throne of hair. But now the frayed ends were always kept in one long braid on one side. The nurse, Patricia, did her hair now so for convenience it was braided out of the way. She also used to look like a princess, she had long fingers and nails and plump cheeks, but in the past few months, she had a face like a skull. Her bones in her fingers stuck out like knobs and her cheeks were almost painful to look at. I used to remember more of her details, like her smell and her true laugh. But over the past few months, she only smelt like the harsh cleaning products they made me use. Her laugh was small now, she would only be able to get out a few giggles before grabbing at her bony face to recover or choking on the laugh and entering a coughing fit that usually ended with my dad rushing around to relieve her. I studied her today, somehow she was more boney and pale than the day before. Each day her and her healthy memories seemed further away. She still kept her same bright smile while I entered. No matter the details, her smiling eyes remained unchanged all this time. No matter how alien the rest of her features became, her eyes when I came in the room were a constant.

I passed between the bed and the dresser, at a calm even pace I could still feel my dad in the hallway. I made my way to my corner, the distance of the corner from my mom made it so I could see her even if she was lying down. Today she was upright so I dragged my chair closer to the bed; I heard little noises coming from the doorway and looked up to see my dad shaking his head at me. This was his way of informing me that I had to stop what I was doing.

"She's fine, I can see her and she's not on anything," my mom interjected but I still slowed and left my chair in its new resting place.

I looked down, just at the base of the bed there are cables and cords all over the floor. Some go under the bed some curl up and go up the wall toward those beeping machines, and others seem to just be tangled up with no beginning or end.

I sat down and my dad almost closed the door leaving just a line of bright light from the hallway across the floor. Now we were in the dull light of the room, the blinds were closed and only a little bit of sunlight seeped in and made bright lines on the opposite side of the room. Somehow these two sets of lines seemed to imprison me every time I was in there. I snapped up from examining the lines and looked to my mom who was repeating her question, "So what do you feel

11

like drawing for me today?" she said pushing herself up further to lean toward where I sat in the middle of the open space.

"I'm gonna draw the dog we're gonna get," I exclaimed now that I felt excited to see her. No matter how much of a stink I put up, she always melted away my annoyance and made me feel special. I imagined in my head the picture, opened the construction paper booklet, and thumbed to the page with the lightest color I could find, yellow.

"We're getting a dog?" She smiled and asked.

"Dad said maybe one day..." I explained, starting on the dog's head. I felt the concentration set in closing the room out and no longer heard the repetitive noises or smelled that horrible scent that filled this room. I could feel her watching me and that was all I was aware of anymore.

As I finished the dog I held it up for my mom but when I looked at her she was almost laying down now. I could only see half her face; she smiled and lifted her head slightly. I walked toward the bed with my artwork held high above my head. I looked at the thin faded line on the floor that marked how close I could come to her bed. Careful not to cross it I pushed the drawing as close as I could to her until she perked up just enough that I could see the effort. She smiled at my masterpiece.

"What's his name?" she asked, trying to lean up closer, fighting with her own weight on the bed.

"Brownie, because he's brown and he likes brownies."

"He likes brownies? That sounds like someone else I know" She laughed and leaned further toward the edge then winked at me.

I laughed and announced, "I'm going to draw his toys."

I laid down on my stomach this time with my picture of Brownie and began adding to the empty space around him. After a little while, my dad came in with a juice box and another glass of water for my mom.

"How are my girls doing?" he asked setting down the water and bending over to leave me the juice box.

"I'm showing Mommy our dog Brownie," I said without looking up or collecting the juice.

"Did you want me to bring in a game?" he asked without even glancing at my drawing.

My dad always suggested games. I hated it, I had to roll for my mom and move my mom's piece if we played anything with dice. It was like I was playing by myself. Card games were not so bad but it usually made her have to cut everything short because she always started to feel sick or tired. Usually, my dad wouldn't offer card games as an option anymore anyways.

"No. I can draw more," I said reaching blindly for my juice that sat in front of me.

"Honey she's fine, can you just get me one more..." she trailed off motioning to the dresser with her eyes.

I heard my dad sigh; he went over to the dresser and shook out one of the various pills. That drew my attention, whenever he had to get her one of the pills while I was in here it seemed she would either fall asleep or feel too sick to have me stay much longer. I turned over my picture of Brownie now complete with a stick, a bone, a ball, and a swimming pool.

"Look Brownie is going to need a pool! It's going to be our favorite toy together and I'm going to teach him how to swim," I announced holding the picture up again for them both to see. I watched my mom make a squinting face while she swallowed the pill with some water then brushed my father's arm. He stared at her with his usual worried expression.

"A dog and a pool?" she squinted at me then smiled at my dad "Sounds like a plan to me."

"Perfect." My dad returned his gaze after rolling his eyes to my mom then shrugging his shoulders.

Her smile remained and she turned down to me again.

"You are an excellent swimmer," she reminded me holding out her hand for the drawing.

"Do you see the pool?" I asked when she aimed the drawing so my dad could see too.

"Yes looks like you both will be swimming up a storm in the summer," she said brushing her hand across my artwork.

This brought me back, my picture of Brownie was hers now and I won't get to hang it on the fridge or in my room. I decided not to draw anymore today, if I just color those pieces they won't get confiscated.

I laid back on my stomach and hummed opening the coloring book that I had received as a bribe to come to her room instead of arriving on time to a friend's birthday party. Since I was going to be around other people my visit had to be before the party. But my mom was with the nurse most of the morning so by the time I went in, we were already late to Annie's birthday.

I had only colored two of the pages so far so I thumbed through until I found one of a ladybug on a leaf, "Should I do this one next Mommy?" I asked. My mom was already slumped back onto her pillow. She held her hand up to her necklace as she usually did and watched me over the edge of her bed. I started on the ladybug with the almost unused red crayon from the box. This crayon still had a completely untouched tip, most of the time I stuck to bright happy colors so the red had little use. I heard her ask my dad to put the drawing of Brownie with the others and I focused on the edge of the ladybug wing.

Chapter Three

THE DAY OF

I heard my fork clatter to the floor while my grandpa was cleaning up from breakfast. Today early in the morning the nurse who goes in my mom's room had visited before the sun had come up and taken my mom somewhere. My dad woke me up and left me with grandpa saying he would be back later. I watched him leave my dark room into the bright hallway through sleepy eyes. I squinted against the light and saw my solemn grandpa hug my dad before patting his back several times. I could see his lips moving but heard no words leave his mouth. The door shut and the sliver of light disappeared. I heard their feet move about outside my room then the light sneaked back in my room making way to a figure. My grandpa closed the door behind him and crossed my room to my bed where he sat on the edge before laying back next to me. I could hear his joints cracking when he pushed off his tiptoes to ensure he did not wake me.

Grandpa cuddled up on my bed with me until the sun finally rose in the sky. Then it hit me. It's Sunday and on Sundays we have pancakes. I jumped from the bed and reminded grandpa before running from the room. I heard him stretch and shuffle behind me. I started to pull the ingredients from the shelves and the pan from under the oven.

He helped me put my special apron on then he crossed the kitchen and yawned before putting the items in a line to start our pancakes.

I usually was allowed to make the batter, pour a few and only on rare occasions flip them on the pan. One time I flipped the pancake right into the fan above the stove and it took my dad a few hours to clean it off. So now I get to flip the small already cooked pancakes. I stood eager to help, but I just watched grandpa start to make the batter. He stared blankly at the bowl and didn't respond when I kept pressing to let me mix and let me measure. He finished the batter and carried the bowl to the pan that was heating on the stovetop. He dropped the first blob in the pan and I continued to protest that I wanted to do it.

Once the batter hit the hot pan he muttered under his breath dashing across the kitchen to grab a spatula to separate the burning pancake from the pan. He scraped the bits onto a pile on the counter. The charred pieces and liquid batter made a small steaming mountain that I stared at a long moment while he went in the fridge for the butter.

Once he lowered the heat and put the butter on the pan he stared straight ahead. I continued to beg him to let me help. Almost as if he was unable to hear me, I pleaded and pulled at his sweat pants. Without warning, he broke from his trance and I straightened up ready to get involved with the pancakes but then he just scooped batter again and let the lumpy batter hit the pan. I continued to protest and promised I was getting better at pouring but he only stared at the bubbling pancakes and flipped each one with no response to my pleading. He ignored me cooking our breakfast in silence.

I pulled off my apron and ceremoniously returned it to its hook on the wall. Turning on the spot to stomp to my chair at the table. I complained about how dad always lets me make the batter and start the first pancakes now. I watched the back of him while he finished the first batch and plated the pancakes before walking the tower to me. I sat with my arms folded as he delivered them and stared at the steaming pile with my face squished into an angry grimace. He went back to the batter and pan to finish the batch and seemed to ignore my reaction. I sat there smelling the sweet buttery freshly cooked pancakes; I caved and climbed down from my chair to fetch the bottle of syrup from our pantry. I smothered the stack before tearing at the tower with the edge of my fork. The pancakes were still hot and still had a small bit of batter in the center. I didn't say anything, it seemed Grandpa wasn't listening anyway. I sat quietly, ate my breakfast, and watched grandpa cook his pancakes and take a seat across from me.

I had just finished the last bite of pancake on my plate and he grabbed the syrup covered crumbs along with his plate that still had all three pancakes, untouched. He put the dishes on the counter turning and knocking the fork to the floor. The fork clattered and he just stood there for a second with vacant eyes staring at the silverware on the floor in front of him. I circled the counter and handed the sticky fork to my Grandpa. He finally broke his stare with the floor, took the fork from my outstretched hand then made a small smile before saying "Go put on some shoes, we have to get going." He dropped the whole stack in the sink, ignored the dirty pan on the stove, and now cooled burnt pancake drying to the kitchen counter. He looked down at me expectantly after he turned around.

"But I'm still in PJ's," I said dancing around showing how the dress twirled when I spun.

"It's fine, today can be PJ day and you can show your mom when we see her."

"We are going to see her? Where is she?" I asked all at once. I was more curious now since last time she was taken out of the house I didn't get to see her at all for days until she showed up again with more machines than before next to her in bed.

"She's at the hospital," he said now in a whisper "she wasn't feeling well so her nurse brought her to the hospital with your daddy."

"So we are going to see her at the hospital?" I asked when he ushered me down the hall.

"Yes, we are going to help her feel better so she can come home."

"OKAY" I jumped up and down and then sprung to run down the rest of the hallway to the door where my shoes were all lined up. I grabbed the pink ones with green and yellow flowers on them. I wasn't supposed to wear them out of the house anymore because they aren't for cold weather.

As I sat on the floor squeezing each foot in I thought about how they always made me feel better so I thought it would work for my mom too. When my grandpa helped me in my jacket and walked me toward the car I smiled, I got away with it—I'm wearing the flower shoes I thought. I missed these shoes, even though they hurt a little now since my feet grew since I last wore them. I just love these shoes they remind me of butterflies and the summer and I was so glad I was going to get to show them to my mom. She only saw them once right after we bought them. I was so excited to show her the shoes that day, I held them up to her then put them on and danced around my corner of her room. She thought they looked like summer too.

I stared down at my shoes and my grandpa put me in the car, buckling my seatbelt. Kicking right then left then right

19

again watching the flowers shake a little with each kick. Grandpa shut the door and stopped for a minute. He turned his back to me and answered his cell phone. I went back to watching my shoes and dancing flowers. I could hear him mumbling and long pauses where all I could hear was the rubber of my shoes hitting my seat before grazing the chair in front of me. I was pulled away from my dancing flower shoes when grandpa opened my door again. He began to unbuckle me. Oh no, he saw my shoes I panicked bending both my knees tight and tried to keep my pink flower shoes out of sight.

He still continued to unbuckle me and when I looked at his face he had tears in his eyes.

"Grandpa, are you crying?" I asked.

"It's okay kiddo, we are just going to stay home a little bit longer," he said lifting me from the seat and carrying me back to the house. When we walked away I noticed he left the door to the car open.

"I can change my shoes. I know I can't wear these when it's cold out." I somewhat cried, I just wanted to see my mom now. I felt myself start to panic, he carried me and ignored my pleading.

He opened the door to the house and put me down. Still he didn't respond to me at all. Ignoring my protests he just continued into the kitchen. He grabbed the phone and began to dial. Speaking to himself with his back to me, he paced our kitchen.

Suddenly he stopped pacing and turned to face me his mouth was open but he wasn't making any noise. He looked down at me and cleared his throat, "Do you want to watch a movie?" he asked staring toward the television in our living room. Placing the phone down without ending the call before escorting me to the television. He turned it on and the last movie I was watching 'The Little Mermaid' came on.

"Grandpa, I just watched this one," I complained from behind him in the kitchen but he continued to talk on the phone.

He twisted to me and bent down, I could see tears balancing on his eyelashes, "Just go watch the movie I will join you in a minute."

I dragged my feet, the rubber pulling at the carpet in the living room. I sat down and removed the shoes one at a time. I put them on the floor in front of me and listened to my movie, staring at my shoes. Eventually, I curled up on the couch and sank under the large blanket that we usually left hanging on the edge of the couch. I must have fallen asleep because the next thing I knew I woke up in my room to grandpa offering me lunch, he kept his eyes fixed on the bedding around me throwing out different options for me to eat. He ran through a long list with his eyes fixed on everything in the room but me:

"Macaroni and cheese, grilled cheese, fish sticks and fries, pizza bagels..." he paused running out of ideas. I sat there watching him ponder other options. "Spaghetti with sauce, vegetable soup, cereal."

"CEREAL" I shouted the second I heard the words leave his mouth. He nodded and left the room. I could tell he was relieved he didn't have to keep coming up with ideas.

I jumped up from the bed to follow him into the kitchen excited about my lunch choice. I crossed in front of my mom's room and I paused before calling up to him a few steps ahead of me "Can we see mom after lunch?"

He paused for a second then continued to walk without answering me. I heard a squeak come from his throat but no words.

I took that to mean no and felt my pace slow, now cereal wasn't so exciting anymore.

After lunch my grandpa kept me busy, we pulled out all my dress up clothes then he played Candyland on the floor with me. After I beat him at Candyland he sat with me and I showed him my stuffed dog that had puppies and recited each of their names. He let me watch another movie, this time I got to pick it and he even let me have the cookies we can only have after dinner. We played in the living room all day and I stayed in my PJ's until we heard a car pull in the driveway. Grandpa stood up with his joints cracking one after the other. I listened to each pop and thought about how he had been on the floor with me for hours. He walked to the window and peered out.

"Is Mommy coming home now?"

He didn't answer but only turned toward me. He walked to where I was on the floor. Bending down for the remote to shut the television off right before the last scene in the movie. I was about to protest to the sudden change in activities but was interrupted by him once more.

"Why don't you go in your room and put away the dress up clothes."

I looked back toward the front where the car pulled into the driveway but couldn't see anyone or anything from the living room window without climbing on the TV shelf and I knew not to do that in front of grandpa. So I just scooped up my pile of dress up clothes before walking to my room. My grandpa followed me and shut the door behind me. I got in the room and dumped the pile in the chest where they belonged before crossing the room to my bed. Sitting on the edge of the bed from where I woke up earlier was my stuffed fish, I picked him up and hugged him and let my legs hang off the bed. He didn't really have a formal name but I usually called him Fishie. I started to play our favorite game, I would lay on my back and he would swim around above me and talk to me. I was playing like this for a while because I started to get hungry and it was almost pitch black out my window. I opened the door to find grandpa for dinner. I turned into the kitchen to see grandpa on the phone again and my dad bent over the counter with his head in his hands.

"Daddy" I screamed running to his leg for a hug. He didn't even look down, I felt my grandpa peel me away from my dad's leg and lift me up. This time when I saw grandpa, tears were soaking his face.

"What's wrong?" I asked when he held me closer and put my head below his so I couldn't see his face. He carried me back to my room and sat me on the bed. Once I was facing him he sighed deeply and asked me if I wanted to have dinner in my room and watch something.

"Yes!" I screamed, completely forgetting all about my grandpa's teary eyes. I'm never allowed to eat in my room and especially not allowed to watch TV with dinner. I ran to the chair for my tea set and got ready for my special dinner and a movie. He turned and headed back to the kitchen to rejoin my dad. I felt my excitement ebb, my curiosity and concern grew. For some reason, my dad was frozen in the kitchen and my grandpa was crying, or had cried. I sat there waiting for him to return and felt as though I was frightened but I didn't know what I was scared of. I could feel this uneasiness with all of the events of today growing. I tried to hide it when I heard his footsteps return. There was something going on and no one wanted to tell me.

23

My grandpa came back with cereal and milk, again. He smiled motioning for me to sit back in my chair, poured me a bowl and set the tablet at the end of the table with cartoons pulled up on the screen. He hit play and put the bowl on the edge of the table closest to me. With that, he turned and left the room. I sat staring at the cereal at first, I am usually only allowed a bowl or so a week but today I had two. I scooped up my first spoonful awestruck at what I was allowed today, first it was cookies, then hours of TV, then cereal twice in one day, now I had my cartoons in my room. That was a huge no-no. *The whole day was just unfolding the weirdest events,* I thought. Then I looked to my closed door, what was happening on the other side of that door? Somehow I knew I shouldn't go investigate just yet. My dad and grandpa didn't seem ready to tell me.

This wasn't the first time my mom was moved for a while. In the past when I would ask, everyone would tune me out. By this point I knew just to wait and everything would go back to normal. But this time things seemed a little different somehow. I returned to my cartoons and crunchy cereal, wiggling in my seat half excited and half scared with the uneasiness that bubbled up in me.

After the cartoon was done and my bowl was just purple colored milk with small crumbs in it, I decided it was time to play swimmies. No one was there to cut me off or tell me '5 minutes, that's it' so I took advantage. I picked up the device and walked to my bed and I clicked on the small square with a picture of three fish with bubble letters that read 'swimmies' underneath. I laid on my bed and started the game where I left off the last time I played. The volume was loud but still no one came in to give me a count down or take away the tablet. Usually, when I played this game I would have a limit or they would only allow me to play in special circumstances. I grinned when I thought about how I got to play the game without the usual restrictions. I sat and played level after level until I felt my eyelids grow heavy.

At some point I fell asleep, the next thing I knew I woke up to my dad holding the tablet and cleaning up the bowl that was still sitting on the small table. "Hey, Daddy," I said looking at the window. It was still pretty dark. "Is it morning?"

He paused with the tablet and bowl balanced in one hand.

"No not yet," he whispered, "Go back to sleep sweetie." I noticed that I was tucked into bed in the same PJ's I had worn all day. I wanted to ask about mom but I felt myself slip back to sleep, I could just hear the metal click of the door closing behind him.

Chapter Four

THE NECKLACE

The next morning I woke up on my own and ran to my dad's room. Usually he would wake me to get ready for school, it must be early if I woke up before him. I was hoping it was still early enough so I could snuggle with him in bed until his alarms work up. But in his room, his bed was made and he wasn't in there. "Daddy?" I called out into his room. The bathroom door was open and the light was off. Then I heard plastic and rattling from my mom's room. I ran down the hallway, turned into her open room and screamed "Mommy!" Startling my dad, he dropped pill bottles and the bag he was holding.

"Honey," he blurted out turning to face me in the doorway.

I looked around the room, the sheets were removed from my mom's bed, the curtains were open and blinds pulled up making it the brightest I have ever seen my mom's room. I continued to follow the wall to all the machines that were no longer lined up in a neat row and not beeping like they usually did. The screens were dark and the wires were meticulously coiled at the base of each towering device. I turned back to face the dresser where my dad squatted and saw he was piling the pill bottles into a white plastic bag one rattling container after the other.

"Is she still at the hospital?" I asked pausing in the door to my mom's room, waiting to be ushered out to wash my hands. After a moment I crept across the threshold into the bright silent room. When I wasn't stopped I walked to the foot of her bed and waited for a response.

My dad was still collecting the bottles he dropped earlier and continued to stare at the floor in front of him. He slowly stood back up with what seemed to be the weight of the room on his shoulders. He never reached his true height his body curled over making him look shorter in this moment.

"No," he said almost too soft to hear him while he put the bag and its rattling contents on the dresser.

"Can I see her?" I asked tracing the outline of the edge of the mattress with my eyes "Where is she?" I pressed further studying my dad still staring at the floor.

He turned and walked to me then sat on the bed. He patted the space next to him and waited. I approached the bed and paused at the thin faded line on the floor, the line that designated how close I could get to her bed. I crossed the line while staring at my dad waiting for a reaction. He continued to pat the space next to him watching my feet. I closed the space between us and hopped up on the spot he was patting.

"We can't see your mom," he started before he covered his mouth and looked at the machines all pulled out from their positions against the wall. He wiped his hand from his face let it slap his leg when he put it down "Your mom isn't with us anymore."

I started to feel sad wondering where she would go. "Where is she?"

27

"Do you remember grandma?" He asked looking at me for the first time. His eyes were pleading for me to agree.

His face was patterned with red marks and his eyelashes were wet. The skin under his eyes was puffy and folded in where it met the skin on his cheeks. If it weren't for his familiar eyes, I wouldn't recognize him to be my dad. While I studied his face he shifted his weight to curl his body closer to mine, he waited for my response. "Kinda," I said thinking of my few blurry memories with grandma.

"And how we had to bury grandma," he continued.

I thought of the time we took a limousine to the graveyard and stood around a white box while people spoke and cried. I remember them putting the box in the ground and mom and dad would always tell me that from now on when we wanted to see her or talk to her we could go here and talk to the grey rock that read Erin Rachel Marshall. The rock had some dates and flowering details along the edges. I used to trace the flowery design with my fingers when we would bring flowers to her.

We used to visit every once in a while until my mom got sick, since then we hadn't gone back.

"Is she with grandma?" I asked picturing another box going in that same hole with grandma. I felt sad and confused since we hadn't spoken about grandma in so long. I studied his face hidden behind his hands. My dad now covered his whole face with his hands and sniffed hard. He's crying, my dad was crying.

"Yes, she's with grandma" he said through his hands wiping his face and nose on the sleeve of his shirt.

"Mom says not to do that," I exclaimed remembering when I would rub my nose on my sleeves and she would send me to get tissues. I ran from the room and got a tissue from bathroom. On my way back I could hear my dad sniffling and moving around on the mattress. Once I was got back in the room he was sitting on the floor with his back against the bed now. I handed him the tissue I just collected and waited for him to say thank you.

After a few moments, I sat down next to him and rubbed his shoulder and said "It's okay, Daddy." He balled up the tissue and put it up on the bedside table. When his arm came back down something silver fell down next to him. He looked over his leg and cleared his throat. He picked up the silver string with care and let the shiny end swing in the light. I watched the string and object swing through the air until he brought the twinkling shape in front of my face.

He let out an eerie chuckle and we watched the silver dance in front of me.

"Do you know what this is?" he asked me. I watched the little heart swing back and forth, it hung even with my gaze now.

"It's Mommy's necklace," I responded. I continued to focus on the heart hanging from the silver string

"Yes, it's Mommy's necklace," he paused sniffling again and he turned his body to face me "And you know what? She wanted you to have it."

"Really?" I asked reaching for the small heart. Her necklace was always around her neck and I could only see the heart shape. Now the silver heart wasn't just a heart but what looked like two bundles of sticks bent and tied together in such a way that they created a heart.

He let the whole necklace collect in my hand, handing me this piece of my mother. I looked at the little twig-like branches that made up the heart and ran my finger over where they all met at the bottom. I thought of this necklace always hanging from her neck. "I get to keep it forever?" I asked looking up at him.

"Yes, and you can think of her every time you wear it." He explained glancing at a purple box that was in the corner of the room with a plastic bag piled on top of it. I looked at the purple box and realized I'd never seen this in here before. The box was on the side of the room with the equipment. I'm never allowed near the equipment so I figured that to be why I never noticed it before. I looked back at the necklace that was in my hands following the long chain to the small silver clasp.

"Okay, I will," I said fighting with the small circle on the chain, "How do I put it on?"

My dad broke his stare from the purple box and turned to face me. "You might be a little young to wear it right now" he noted lifting the chain from my hand "Let's find a safe place to keep the necklace in your room until you're a bit older."

I was going to protest, I wanted to put it on now but he was already on his feet beside me.

He put his hand out for me to hold. We walked down to my room and hung the necklace from a picture of my mom and dad that sat on my tall dresser. I could still see the heart under the light but it was too far for me to get to. I felt myself get sad thinking about waiting to wear the necklace.

"Do you want to help me make some breakfast?" he asked touching my mom's face on the frame before turning to look at me.

"Cheesy Eggs?" I asked studying his face again. He was now a little more composed and brighter. He took a breath and nodded to my request.

The two of us left the room and my attention was pulled to breakfast. He made his way down the hallway with me hopping behind him chanting "Cheesy eggs, cheesy eggs, cheesy eggs." When we walked by my mom's room he paused and turned into the room. I continued to hop toward him, unaware of his pause, until I bumped into his butt. While I waited behind him, he leaned his upper body in without allowing his feet to cross the threshold. He grabbed the doorknob and swung his upper body with it closing the door to her room. He then continued with a slower pace to the kitchen I heard him let out one long breath before plastering a strange looking smile on his face and announcing "Cheesy egg time." He motioned for me to get my apron that hung next to the fridge. I searched the counter for our pancake mess from yesterday but he must have cleaned it up so I ran and put the loop over my head then pulled the strings behind my back. I can tie but I still can't tie this behind my own back.

I walked over to my dad "Can you tie it?" I asked and he looked down making a face at my apron. The front of my apron, that I got this past year for Christmas read, 'I'm a great cook just like Mommy'. I watched his face frown and his eyes begin to gather tears. He cleared his throat and motioned for me to turn around. I turned around and felt the letters of Mommy on my stomach. Tracing them with my fingers while keeping my elbows tight so my dad could tie the apron around my back. He finished the bow and sniffled again before standing back up and walking toward the fridge. "Should we make bacon too?" he asked interrupting my focus on following the embroidered Y on the apron.

"Bacon!" I shouted back tracing the embroidered word for the third time. I watched my dad collect ingredients and put the pan on the stove. When his back was turned I walked back down the hallway, I started to feel sad that I couldn't see my mommy anymore.

31

When he first was explaining about how this was like Grandma I could feel his lips tighten at the end of every word, he did not want to discuss what happened anymore. For as long as my mom had been sick he had not wanted to talk to me or explain anything so I usually waited to intercept information through hearing him talk to the nurse or grandpa. So I was used to his short answers and code responses, now that he had his back turned I felt my sadness grow and thought about her sweet face and loving smile, I missed her already.

Without instructing my feet toward her room. My legs carried me down the hall to her, I walked in silence to the space right before her door. I turned to my mom's room and reached up to open the door then peered into the bright room. I stood there continuing to trace the word Mommy on my stomach with my other hand.

The room was so quiet and it was too bright. It seemed so different without the beeping, the hum of all the equipment, and blinds blocking all natural light leaving only a small lamp to light the room. There was not enough noise and too much light now. I thought about how it was before, the loud dim room that contained my Mom. Now it was the quiet bright room that missed her. Until that morning, I never knew that the light and quiet I craved to have here came with such a heavy trade. My eyes squinted at the light and my ears rang with the silence broken only by my shuffled steps into her room. She wasn't here anymore.

I imagined her lying on the bed like she normally did and walked over to my corner. I pulled out a piece of construction paper and a crayon and started to draw the first thing I thought of, the necklace. I drew the long round chain then a frayed heart with tiny little branches. I finished the drawing and carried my newest artwork to her bed. I paused watching for the cords. When I looked down there were none around the bed. I looked up on the empty bed and put the picture where her head would rest. I took a few steps back and could hear my dad pulling out plates in the kitchen. "Emma, I thought you were going to help me?" he asked and I heard dishes clatter.

I looked at the corner of the drawing balanced on her bed. "Thank you for the necklace Mommy, it's really pretty." I paused and I pictured her sitting in her usual spot on the bed "I miss you." I told her bed, I felt a lump in my throat grow and threaten to silence my voice. "I love you." I squeezed out and the lump took over and grew into tears on my face. I shuffled from her room shutting the door behind me before swallowing hard to return to my dad. Once I was back in the kitchen, I wasn't hungry.

In the kitchen my dad was putting a full plate at my seat at the table.

"Here you go Emma Bemma," he said sniffling again and keeping his face from my line of sight. I came up behind him and hugged his legs and let myself break. I cried holding the back of his legs until he picked me up and we both cried together. None of the cheesy eggs or bacon was eaten, we just sobbed with each other until we couldn't anymore.

Chapter Five

SUMMER CAMP

I sat in the backseat of the car, silent. I could feel my dad searching for something else to say to me.

"I still don't see why I have to go, I have friends here I want to see them," I protested again crossing my arms and looking out the window.

We were just entering the next town and starting this forty-minute drive to some camp. I was being sent there for 14 days. Two weeks. Two weeks at this place that boasts so much to do, new people to meet, and s'mores. I already felt my boredom setting in, the pictures in the pamphlet were obviously staged and this was going to be two weeks of torture, with s'mores. The worst part was I thought I would spend all summer with my friends and Brownie, I signed everyone's yearbooks about my excitement to go to the mall every day, go swimming at the beach, and have sleepovers all summer. That made the sting of learning my dad's plan that much worse. All the anticipation I had for the summer that awaited me was for nothing. It was about to be the worst summer ever. This place did not have any of my friends and no one I even knew was going. I found out on the last day of school that he signed me up and I would have to pack for my departure, since that conversation I have been fighting to stay home. I know it's only two weeks but summer vacation flies by and I'm going to miss so much in those fourteen days. By the time I'm back my friends might have all new inside jokes that leave me out. I don't want to spend the rest of the summer on the outside of some hilarious joke.

Either way, I was signed up and now it was time to go to this stupid camp. The night before I was arguing back and forth with my dad until he did his classic 'and that's final'.

We stood between the kitchen and living room shouting at each other while I tried to convince him how much I would miss my friends and Brownie. "I'm not going and you can't make me," I shouted while I stood there and stared at him, each time we spoke our voices would rise a little louder. This time knew it was louder hearing the fancy plate on our wall shudder at my volume.

During fights like this, I would imagine my mom being on my side, this always made me miss her more.

He shot back "I already paid so you're going and that's final" and it echoed in our house. Poor Brownie took this to be his cue to leave and he shuffled into the bathroom at the end of the hall. His personal hiding spot for sporting events, storms, and fights between me and my dad. I stood there fighting back more tears and watched my dad hold his gaze on me. I stomped from the living room, down the hall, past Brownie's hiding spot and into my room. Once I slammed the door I fell to the floor and cried. I made sure to cry loud against the door so he could hear from where he inevitably stood in the kitchen. I was hoping eventually he would crack and not make me go.

I was wrong.

Sometime later my dad knocked and let himself in. He kept encouraging me to pack, which turned into him packing my items in silence. Since then we haven't said anything until I broke the silence in the car.

"You will make new friends at camp and you will love it," he said evenly back to me turning onto the highway.

"But I like my friends and this place looks so weird."

"This is the same place your mom used to go every summer and she loved it. She really wanted you to go too."

"So…" I argued back. *Why would that matter? It's not like she would be there,* I thought. We both took a long moment to speak again, the mention of her still took time to recover. I started to think about the validity of his statement. Why was this the first time he mentioned my mom going to the camp. We both knew it wouldn't change anything, she wasn't here.

"Just try it, if it's that bad after the first week we will talk about bringing you home early," I heard him say over my thoughts of my mother. I could hear the defeat in his voice with this suggestion.

"Fine." I shot back in his direction before I turned and watched the trees go by out the window. Perfect, all I had to do was wait a few days and call him in tears and he would end this early. I continued to daydream and watched the endless green of trees flash by, perfecting my plan on when and how to cut this whole summer camp thing short.

I was pulled back from my scheming when he turned down a dirt road with a small wooden sign that read, 'Camp Blue Rock'. I looked down at the clock in the car and did the math, turns out he lied. This place was over an hour away. I made an audible sigh tapping on the plastic clock display and waited for my dad to note my point. He just smiled enthusiastically happy to have succeeded in getting me to the camp. I rolled my eyes and refocused out the window watching the entrance and parking lot that were in chaos. Everyone was being dropped off with several bags and pillows and all sorts of stuff. I had one bag and I wasn't even sure what was packed in there due to my own stubbornness. I tried to look annoyed while my dad packed the bag so not once did I look to see what he actually put for me.

My dad found an open spot and turned the car off quickly hopping out. He didn't want to give me one more second to complain. I pulled at the door handle and slid to the gravel before meeting him at the truck to collect my belongings. I had a pillow and pillowcase so I looked like the other girls, but I didn't act like them. Girls were waving to each other and hugging to celebrate being reunited, I stood there alone and annoyed. I watched them all say goodbye to their moms and dads making deals with their parents on how many letters they promise to send home.

Turns out in addition to no TVs, this place also had no phones except for emergencies. I looked around and heard someone come over and ask my name. I pretended not to hear and stood there hugging my pillow staring down at the line that marked the outer edge of our parking spot. I heard my dad respond, "Emma Peterson."

Then I heard her rustling papers and repeating my name over and over until "Ah hah, you're in Squeaking Squirrels" she told me handing me a purple cutout of a squirrel made of some kind of rubber. The small animal had a little hole cut out, I would assume for a keychain, I tucked it into my palm against my pillow. The counselor explained where to go, I tuned her out and watched the girls running up the hill toward the brown cabins tucked into the trees.

I heard my dad say "Alright." He picked up my bag and started in the direction she just explained. I followed behind and refolded my arms across my chest with my pillow squished under them. We walked to the second to last house that had a familiar purple squirrel painted at the apex of the roof with the words Squeaking Squirrels carved into the wood by the door. To get into the house there were four creaking wooden steps, a short deck, and then a squeaky door. *This place was falling apart,* I thought to myself frowning.

I shot my dad a look "It's the same as when mom was here too apparently," I said making a face nodding toward the cracks in the floor. I pushed the door open to reveal a room with dim light that was absorbed by the dark cabin walls. The room was already filled with girls chatting, laughing, and unpacking. When I walked into the room another woman in a green hat came rushing toward me.

"Welcome to Squeaking Squirrels. I'm Veronica but everyone calls me 'V'" she announced. "What's your name?" she asked smiling at me, making sure I could see all the way back to her molars.

"Emma" I told her glancing around to see the other girls in the cabin. Hoping to find one familiar face in the crowd to improve my mood.

"Emma Peterson," She confirmed and she made a check on her sheet. I could see a dozen or so other checks on the page showing how many other girls had already arrived. I wanted to roll my eyes at how late we were, but I could feel her watching me again.

"Great you're our last one," she announced and she turned to face the one open bunk. It was the top bunk, closest to the creaking door. I looked up at the bed then to my dad.

He didn't seem to think hopping on this bed was an inconvenience so he just tossed my bag up there and said "Great, looks like you're all set honey," he turned to hug me and I just stood there in horror. "Why don't you get yourself introduced and I'll get out of your hair," he said fluffing up my hair.

I just narrowed my eyes at him and let him hug me one more time before turning and walking out the door, down the steps and onto the noisy gravel sidewalk at the end of our horrible cabin. I turned to face the woman who had pointed me to this bunk. She started with introductions, pointing to the other woman in a green cap before circling the room with the other girls who were just about done unpacking. *Great, not only was I the last one, but they are all settled in and I still don't even know what's in my bag,* I thought. I was so busy contemplating my bag I didn't hear one name in her introductions so I just nodded and waved to the girls across the way and shared an awkward smile with the girl under my bunk. I will be sleeping on this girl for the next thirteen nights and I missed her name, I'm already counting the seconds until I get to leave this place.

After our counselor was satisfied with introductions she adjusted her green cap and walked back toward her bunk, I climbed up onto my bed and started to unpack my bag while the others talked about where they were from and what they wanted to do first at the camp. I listened for any activities that might actually interest me but was let down again. So far most of the girls were picking positions for basketball or other sports. I did hear someone mention a swim test so they can go on the slide and water trampoline that made my ears perk up. I recalled seeing these in the photos. *Oh no, did my dad even pack me a suit?*

I started to pull out the items packed in the bag one by one and stacked them in neat piles beside me on the bed while taking inventory. So far I have ten shirts, eleven pairs of shorts (thanks dad because I'll just go topless that last day), one hoodie, one pair of flip-flops plus the sneakers I wore here, and one bathing suit. I saw the suit and felt my body get less tense. At least I know one activity I can do. I continued to pull items from the bag, some more tops (so maybe he did know I needed shirts), three pairs of pants, my toiletry bag, and my undergarment bag that I shuddered thinking of my dad packing for me. At the bottom there was a towel, sheets for my bed, and a wrapped gift between it all. I paused at this discovery feeling a pang of guilt.

The gift was wrapped in tissue paper, because my dad still hadn't mastered wrapping, and tied together with a green ribbon. It was tied in a nasty knot, again because my dad still hadn't mastered wrapping. I fought with the ribbon but it just seemed to stretch and cut into my fingers. I started to pull the stretched ribbon toward the corners of the hard box but couldn't pull it far enough before my finger started to turn white and threatened to bleed. I flipped the whole thing over to come at it from another angle. I was pulled away when I saw my new bunkmate standing eye level with my gift. I turned to face her and she announced "Hold on, I'm a girl scout." She bent down to her bag and came up with a small pocketknife. "Always be prepared" she announced holding the open knife to me.

I reached for it and whispered "Thanks," wondering how long she had been watching me. I cut the ribbon, replaced the knife, and held the pocketknife to her. Turning the knife I saw an inscription on the long edge 'Brittney'. *Perfect now I know at least one person's name here,* I thought and she took the knife from my hand.

"You already have a care package?" She asked throwing the knife back into her bag.

"Yeah, I guess," I responded pulling at the ribbon from the gift and unrolling the items from the tissue. I could feel her eyes on me while I separated a slim silver case, small white box, and drawing pad. On the first page, there was a note from my dad.

Emma Bemma,

Hope you have fun at your first summer camp! I will be missing you so much at home. Don't forget to put on bug spray and write home when you can. I put some cash in the tin here for stamps and whatever else you want to buy at the store while you're there. I love you so much.

Love,

Dad

P.S. I thought this would be the best time for you to wear your mom's necklace. She got the necklace just before going to camp. Take care of it and think of your mom. She will always love you.

I stared at the note, the necklace? I kind of remember him giving me the necklace when I was little but right after it was put away for 'safe-keeping'. It was relocated over the years and out of my bedroom so I hadn't thought about her necklace in some time. Now I get to have it? I wondered.

I was pulled away by Brittney scoffing, "Pfffft, no candy or goodies. What's in the boxes?"

I turned and pulled the lid from the silver metal box and out fell two twenty dollar bills.

"Jackpot!" she announced smiling up at me.

Remaining in the box were crisp unused charcoal pencils. I turned them to face her. "I like drawing," I explained returning the lid and put the cash in my pants pocket. I lifted the white box and felt something small hit against the side. I saw most of the other girls from our cabin escape through the door when a bell rang announcing that it was lunchtime. Brittney stayed and watched me open the small white box. I lifted the lid and watched the light from the now open cabin door dance off the silver necklace that sat cushioned on the cotton in the box. I reached in and picked up the silver heart that I remember hanging from my mom's neck in pictures and blurry memories. The chain swung back and forth prompting Brittney to ask "Oh pretty, who is that from?"

I looked down with a pang of guilt. My dad had packed all this up for me and left me the note while I lay on my bed too stubborn to admit defeat. I lifted my face back to the necklace and unhitched the clasp. "My mom," I told her. I felt a smile creep to my face as the words left my mouth.

I pulled the clasp under my hair and met up with the small circle balanced between my fingernails and let the clasp close. I turned back to my gifts and stacks of clothes that were spread out on my bunk. "I'm going to finish getting settled in before lunch," I told her. I wasn't ready to go try to find these strangers at lunch and I wasn't feeling very hungry. I was hoping my explanation would get her to stop watching me. It was starting to make me hyper-aware of all the items on my bed.

"Don't take too long, you don't want to miss lunch," she warned bending to put on her shoes. She stood and hurried out of the cabin. I was so thankful it worked and I was left alone in the dull light of our quiet cabin. I looked around at everyone's spaces and tried to recall the names but there was nothing, I was too lost in my own thoughts at the time. I put my pillow at the top of my bed and fell back onto it. I didn't want to unpack I just wanted to go home and see Brownie and my friends from home. I lay there convincing myself not to cry, I didn't want someone to walk in and see me crying like a baby just moments after being dropped off. I turned to face the wall and felt the silver heart slide down until the chain from my chest landed on my pillow.

There was a flash and I had this weird sensation of being moved. It felt like my bunk was collapsing. I went to put my arms out but felt like I had no control, I felt my head moving without being able to control it. I turned and saw the middle of the cabin. It looked the same but now there were girls clamoring in there, did I fall asleep? I searched their faces not one was familiar. How little was I paying attention before? I was still on my bunk laying back but I could feel sheets on the bunk, did I put them there then fall asleep?

My body started to sit up, what was going on? I sat up and felt my bare legs, I was in shorts? I distinctly remember wearing jeans this morning. The shorts I was wearing now were like a windbreaker material, I don't even remember finding these in my bag? I was also barefoot, when did I take my shoes off? Did I somehow time travel the whole week to the end and it was time to go home?

Without warning, I felt my weight on my hands and my body hopped off the edge of the bunk and landed with a thump on the floor. My body turned to face my bunkmate. She looked oddly familiar but not who I had met just a moment ago.

"Were you ready to go then?" I heard myself say, my voice sounded different and I don't even recall thinking to say anything to her. The girl grabbed a bag of some kind of food then stood up next to me nodding and smacking the gum in her mouth.

Where have I seen this girl before? I thought while my feet slipped into flip-flops and walked me out in front of my new bunkmate. I was greeted by rain bouncing off the railing and splashing my arms and legs. My body continued into the rain and I felt my arms raise up to greet each drop to my skin. I urged myself to cover up. I hated the feeling of cold rain on my bare arms. My body didn't obey and my arms remained lifted welcoming the icy wet drops. I then turned to this new girl and heard myself shout "Race you to our spot!" My body pushed off from where it stood and ran through the cold rain. I felt the slippery flip-flops connecting with the mud. My body took a sharp right and ran behind the cabin and into the woods. I could hear the girl following behind me. We raced to a spot I didn't even know about. My body took me there.

Is this what possession feels like, am I possessed or something? I felt trapped in my own skin. As I felt myself run I noticed that my hair was short and tucked behind my ears. I CUT MY HAIR? Why would I ever do that? I started to hate this camp even more, what happened? Was I just lost in the most realistic dream ever? I pushed my body to wake up but I could feel the cold rain and the dirt under my feet. The mud was separating my feet from my shoes. That slimy feeling was so distinct there was no way I could create that in my sleep. This was too real to be just a nightmare that I could wake myself from.

My body prepared for a leap onto this boulder sticking out of the earth then continued to the edge and balanced between the hard surface and another neighboring oversized rock. I felt my hands touch the cold rough surface. Then I noticed I had chipping nail polish on my fingers. What was going on? My hands barely even looked familiar. My body squeezed between the two rocks then crouched under the overhang. The rain stopped hitting my skin. I could still hear it hitting the leaves and the rocks in front of me but in this little cave, I was protected. I watched my new bunkmate repeat my steps and meet me in the cavern.

"You cheated," she huffed out once we were seated across from each other.

"No, I'm just faster than you" I felt myself say. What was going on with my voice? It sounded different in my own head.

"But you had a head start" she got out lifting the bag before removing a deck of cards tucked in her back pocket. I watched my hands brush leaves and pebbles from the space between where we sat. Urging my muscles to obey and pull my hand away from the slimy wet leaves and gravel. Still they pressed on cleaning the space before slapping together to rub off the dirt that remained on my palms. Once my hands were nearly cleaned off they rested in my lap, while my new bunkmate dealt out the cards. Looking down I noticed my clothes, now soaked, none of these were familiar. None of these were from my closet, never mind the bag my dad packed for me.

She finished and pushed the deck to me I picked it up and started to set up a game of solitaire. I watched my barely familiar hands spread out the cards.

"Rosie, do you want left or right?" the stranger asked.

WHAT, not my name! I sent messages to my brain to correct her. Then I felt myself answer "Left! We always start left."

What is going on, am I stuck in someone else's body? I can't control anything and for some reason, this girl thinks my name is Rosie. I felt my hand rise up to the necklace hanging from my neck. This felt familiar, I remember just putting on the necklace earlier that day. Then I felt my hands go down to the cards and hover there. Without warning, I heard the girl and my strange voice shout in unison, "Ready, set...SPIT!"

My hands moved in what felt like familiar circles placing cards on one of the two piles in the center. I had no idea what we were playing but for some reason my hands did. The two of us slowed until I felt myself say "ready, set, SPIT!" The whole process started again until I placed my last card and slapped the pile on the right. I felt the stranger's hand hit mine, my body laughed and picked up the portion of the deck that it just slapped. This continued while the rain picked up and slowed down, we would talk between rounds and usually my hand would be slapped by hers, I took this to mean that I was winning because my new bunkmate got frustrated each time and my body would celebrate. After some time I think I had won because my hand slapped the rock where there were no cards stacked this round and I made a wahoo sound. The whole process started again, I listened to the rain tinker off and felt the sunlight shine down and touch the top of my foot. My body moved to allow my face to peer out of our cave and I announced "Looks like it's going to stop."

A second later I heard the bell ring and felt my face turn to meet the stranger.

"It's pizza bagel day!" We celebrated in unison climbing out from the overhang; we shook the loose dirt from our clothes and collected the empty snack bag and cards. We walked back to the cabin laughing and talking. I saw the familiar name on the door, but did the purple squirrel fall off in the storm? It didn't sit at the top of our cabin anymore. The cabin looked a little less rattled now; maybe the faded wood looked better once it was wet. Once inside I made my way to the back of the cabin, I watched in the corner of my eye my reflection walk past making my way to the bathroom stall. Now I was confused, my hair was lighter, shorter, and my face looked different. *Great, I am trapped in someone else's body,*

I thought standing back up and walking to the sink to wash my hands. I saw my face in the mirror, *MOM?* I thought once I saw her face. She was younger but it was definitely my mother's face. I studied the frame of her face, she was so young, I've never really seen her this young but it was her face staring back from the mirror. I felt her walk and rejoin the stranger again "Beth, you ready to go?" I was trying to place her face while we stood there, although she looked familiar I couldn't quite figure out where I've seen her before.

We jogged to the dining hall. This looked smaller but was in the same location as the dining hall I saw earlier. I was lost in thought when my mom collected her pizza and salad, filled her cup, and sat with a bunch of girls including the familiar stranger from earlier.

How did I end up in my mom's body? Did I time travel? What is going on?

I continued to try to think, listening to my mom talk and laugh with the girls at her table. She finished her plate and downed the remainder of her water, "Should we start it?" she asked the girl across the table from her. The girl downed her drink and flipped the cup over in her hands to show her assent.

I felt my mother's hands begin to slap the table and the cup, and then turn the cup over, and start the whole pattern over again. The beat spread like a wave down her table and across the whole dining hall until every girl was keeping up with the rhythm. This was so familiar and my mom kept the beat while chanting some song with the others about the camp. I heard them sing about all the cabins including the Squeaking Squirrels, then talk about the lake, the games, and the counselors. At the end, everyone cheered and stopped the cup and hand drumming on the tables.

I felt my mom stand up and move toward the counter covered in dirty dishes, she balanced hers in the mess before turning and walking to the door. She wrapped her arm around the stranger, I now know to be Beth, from earlier. They exited the door and a counselor had stopped them for a photo. My mom squeezed Beth's face to her face and announced "Best friends forever!" smiling for the photo.

After the counselor smiled and moved on to the next set of girls, the two of them walked toward the cabin. My mom hopped on the top bunk by the door, the same one I was placed in when I had arrived. She laid on her stomach and let her hair dangle toward the floor. They made small talk about funny stories from their towns and friends. I heard Beth say the name of her city and it clicked, I recognized the girl. She was in my parents' wedding and used to stay with us from time to time if she visited because she lived over two hours away.

They laughed for a little while longer at each other's stories before my mom paused and she asked Beth "You ready for the lake?" I watched Beth nod with excitement. My mom pulled her body back up onto her bunk and reached for her bag at the end of the bed pushed against the wall.

I felt a rush, the room darkened and I lost sight of the bag. I was just staring at the inside wall of the bunk. I regained control over my arms and pushed myself up. I felt my clothes, the same ones I was wearing earlier. I looked down to my sneakers, which were on my cot wiping dirt on my bag. I probably should have removed them before climbing up here I realized. I looked around the room. It was exactly as I had remembered from earlier. I was still the only one in the cabin. Faintly in the air I could hear a familiar pattern of drumming reach my ears. I hopped down from the bunk turning my ear toward the dining hall. It was the same beat my mom had done a moment ago with her cup. It was a little messier with hands and cups hitting out of step but it was definitely the same pattern. I ran to the dining hall and saw the familiar face of Brittney waving me over to a spot near her at the table. I sat down and the counselor across the way passed me her cup. She continued the pattern with just her hands. "You will catch on quick" she explained nodding for me to watch the others. I picked up the cup and waited for the pattern to loop to the beginning.

"It's the same thing over and over and really easy to learn, watch," Brittney explained to me watching my hands and continuing to keep up with the rest of the girls. I started tapping the cup and the table in the pattern my mom had done earlier. Just when I started to fall in the groove with the other girls I heard the counselors and a few of the girls at our table start the chant. I heard the familiar words, they went through the song and paused before restarting again. When they got to the end the second time the counselors and few girls cheered. A woman with glasses held up her hands in the middle of the room.

"Welcome to week one of Camp Blue Rock" she announced smiling and turning her head like a sprinkler to cover the whole room. "That was our cheer, for those of you returning you should remember. For those of you that are new, we were all new here at one point and we look forward to teaching all of you too."

She nodded at the crowd and smiled before putting her hands above her head "Now let's get this week started!" She said lowering her arms as if starting a drag race. Everyone clapped and disbursed from the dining hall. I followed along and put myself in with the group from my table luckily close beside my bunkmate, Brittney, the most familiar face so far.

We made the trip back up the creaky steps and filed in the doorway. When we walked in girls were chatting about the lake and how the first swim test was in one hour. Brittney asked me "Did you want to take the test too?"

"Yes," I replied reaching around her to my bag to collect my swimsuit and towel.

She pointed at my neck "That looks really pretty. You might want to take it off before you lose it in the lake."

I instinctively reached up and felt my mom's necklace hanging just above my collar. I thought about my memory from earlier with my mom wearing the necklace in the rain. "It should be fine," I said letting my hand drop and starting toward the bathroom to change.

Once Brittney and I were in our suits we hugged our towels over our chests and walked side by side toward the lake.

"Is this your first time here?" Brittney asked.

"Yes, first time at any sleep-away camp," I replied watching the sun dance over the lake.

"Me too. But my mom said I would love it here. How long are you here for?"

"Two weeks," I answered matter-of-factly.

"Me too!" She answered with excitement in her voice. We laid our towels over the fence by the lake taking the cue from the girls who had obviously attended this camp before.

We both looked up to see the slide, diving board, trampoline, boogie boards, and canoes. We met eyes and smiled while we both walked down to the water to join the other girls in the swim test. We all listened to the lifeguard about what was involved in the test and the safety at the lake. I was only half-listening to the points and general rules while I pictured my mom at this same introduction. My dad had mentioned how she went to camp but it didn't seem to matter before I saw her here. Now it felt like I could feel her everywhere I turned. Somehow I felt more excited than ever to enjoy the water, the woods, and the dining hall with these strangers; just like my mom had years ago.

I heard the lifeguard clap her hands together when she finished her spiel. She told us all to begin and then readied her stopwatch that hung around her neck.

Brittney and I ran down to the water with the other girls and jumped in screaming at the temperature. After the initial shock faded we all swam out to the designated area and began the task of treading water for the lifeguard. We went through the rest of the test with the group of girls joking around and talking more to each other when we could.

Everyone that went out passed the swim test. Once we passed, we were given a blue bracelet with black waves printed on it. We were kicked out of the lake until later that day as they had several rounds of the test to administer and a group had already formed on the shore waiting their turn. So we took our time and swam toward the shore talking about all we could come back and do later. Brittney and I toweled off and walked toward the cabin when she asked "Do you want to play cards, my mom told me to bring cards."

I looked at her surprised and excited. Possibly too excited for a game of cards so I turned my face to the floor to hide my over-enthusiasm. "Yeah, yeah I'll play some cards," I paused. "My mom told me about a really cool place to go to play," I told her picturing the small cave that my mom and her friend had played in. It felt odd almost like a lie once the words left my mouth. She didn't quite tell me about it, but it was an exciting secret I had now. Having this flashback to my mother's time here was like a secret memory that no one else knew about or would even be able to understand. "It's pretty close to our cabin too," I explained further realizing I was so lost in thought on my mom that I wasn't sure if she even agreed to come with me.

"Cool," she responded and we walked toward the cabin with our shoes squeaking from the water. I smiled thinking about watching my mom at this same place and couldn't wait to see the cave again. I reached up and felt the heart hanging around my neck still cold from the water. My hair was tangled in the chain so I untangled the back of my neck while we walked up the steps to our cabin. Once inside I reached on my bunk for the clothes I had worn earlier that I had threw up there before the trip to the lake. I watched the clothes slide off the edge into my hands and saw a heart carved into the corner of the bunk near my pillow. The heart was scratched deep into the wood and worn from the many years of girls in this bunk sleeping against its shape. In the heart were three small letters scratched into the wood.

REM

I read the three letters and thought of my mom, I know my mom's maiden name because of my uncle and grandmother. Rose Erin Marshall.

I pictured her in the same cabin and the same bunk etching those letters into the wall. I turned to Brittney who had just returned from changing and was tying her sneakers. "Can I borrow your pocket knife again?" I asked.

She reached into her bag and rustled around until she found the same pocketknife from earlier. "Here you go," she said handing the small knife over to me. I hopped up on my bunk and began to carve my initials under my mom's in the small remaining space of the heart. When I finished the tiny 'P' I smiled and put my hand over the heart, now so thankful I was stuck with this bunk over all the others in the room. I passed the closed knife back over my side to Brittney. "Thanks," I said hopping back to the floor. I stood there a moment admiring the heart with our initials inside smiling to myself. *Looks like this camp was meant to be,* I thought turning and walking to the back to change for a card game I could only assume was called spit.

Chapter Six

She Left Me

My heart raced in my chest on the bus ride home. Every stop brought me closer to the part of my day I had been dreading since this morning.

Every May the same day came up. Mother's Day. Each year I would be forced into some art project or random assignment that would remind me that I was one of the few without a mom. My dad had not remarried and had no intention to. When I was a little younger some of his friends and even our family would try to set him up. Sometimes he would disclose to me that it was a date, but usually I just figured it out based on his general distaste at his plans when he left me with the babysitter.

My mom had a few close friends that used to take me out for girl's days when I was younger and she had just passed. But over the years they had either moved or had children of their own. This made it so that now my only girl's days were with girls my age. So when I was around grownups it was my dad or my grandpa. So every May when we would make our gifts or write to our mothers, I had no one to even force to collect these creations.

Per the instructions from our teachers I used to bring them home, but this ended in disaster one year. That year a particularly creative teacher had us make paper flowers and bring them home from school with a note. My note was empty minus the preprinted 'Dear Mom' at the top. I forgot about the flowers in my bag and my dad unpacked it in the kitchen to get ready for the weekend he found the flowers and note. I remember watching when he fell to the floor in tears. It took a second to realize the catalyst. Once I did, I felt horrible for putting my dad through that.

Since that day I had taken to either disposing of the gifts at school or immediately when I got home. I didn't tell him or advertise this portion of my day when we discussed school. I tried to protect my dad. After all, it was only him and me now.

This year I didn't have to worry about hiding a gift, I had to complete a writing assignment. I glared at the teacher who was punishing me when she detailed the requirements of our assignment and explained the due date was Friday so we had our papers in time for the weekend to give to our mother on Mother's Day. Her efficient plan wasn't really an advantage for me.

I went through the rest of the day angry debating the assignment in my head. Somehow the rest of my classes took it easy on me and this remained my only homework for the day. I willed other assignments to provide a reasonable procrastination tool for me. I was too conscientious to ignore instructions from my teacher and knew that without a viable excuse I would be forced by my own free will to work on this inconvenient paper. The day went on and classes passed all the while I continued to let my mind swirl with the one line of inspiration for our writing assignment.

What you are thankful for, that your mom has done for you?

The bus hissed to a stop, it was too soon. I felt myself rise letting all the other kids at my stop climb out first before shuffling to the door, melting down the steps, and walking to my dad's car. Now that I was in view I tried to contort my expression from worry and defeat to something that rang more exhausted. Hoping that appearing tired would minimize our small talk for the short drive home.

My dad had been able to change his workday so he was there to pick me up from the bus most days but then has to go back to work when we get home. That usually means that I had two to three hours where he was too busy to directly supervise me.

We had a system that I would do my homework at that time so we could both watch TV together after dinner. I was responsible so he rarely checked up on homework and only helped me when I approached him. For some reason today when he picked me up from the bus he wanted to know more than usual about my assignments.

Was it my imagination or did he know? Maybe it was my inability to disguise my despair as exhaustion in an effort to deter the inevitable.

"So do you have a lot of work tonight?" he asked.

"No," I shot back.

"Need any help?"

"No," I shot back even faster, not leaving any room for negotiation.

"Okay, well I am here if you need me."

"Okay," I said with finality, I already knew I wouldn't and couldn't need him.

Once we were home, I sat on the floor untying my shoes and delaying the journey to the table. I could hear him in the kitchen so I was trying to delay any other questions until we parted ways.

Finally, he headed to his home-office and I went to the kitchen table. He had crammed a desk and filing cabinet into his bedroom when he made this arrangement with work. The room my mom used to be in would have made a more suitable fit for his office but neither of us could stand to be in there. He didn't have the heart to make the room a formal guest room, I think seeing a bed in there made it too familiar. Now it was a catch-all for anything without a place. We kept an old stationary bike, a box of stuffed animals, and a dresser filled with our winter clothes and extra towels. If we did have a guest, which was typically grandpa, we had an air mattress but it was only set up for the night. My dad would never prepare the room by inflating it early and he would start deflating it before we even had breakfast. Each time he stayed over I would walk by in the morning and see the deflated rectangle stripped ready to be packaged up in the center of the room. I didn't ever do my homework in there. I preferred the kitchen table so I could have a snack and daydream out the large window across the room.

I circled the table dropping my bag at my seat on the far end. My dad left my snack out since he usually stops home before going to the bus stop. I stared at the bowl with my usual yogurt and granola, no longer hungry.

I knew I was lost in thought for some time when my dad came down to grab some water.

"Not hungry?" He asked surveying the untouched snack and my solemn face.

"Not really" I responded hoping he wouldn't push any further.

He grabbed his glass and started toward the hallway. "I'm here if you need anything, okay sweetie?" he reminded me again pressing a little harder this time. He paused in the doorway smiling expectantly.

He's a mind reader I thought waiting for him to respond with, 'Yes I am.'

But instead he continued out of the room.

After I was alone again I took in a long breath and held it until the air escaped from my lungs, focusing my thoughts. I decided to just bite the bullet.

I pulled out my notebook from writing class and put my name and the title of the assignment in the top right corner. Then I just sat there waiting for further instruction from my brain to reach my hand.

I started thinking of examples the teacher had given, helping with homework, making lunches, teaching us, doing laundry, and bringing us to sporting events or friends' houses.

The more I thought the more annoyed I was. I stared at the untouched snack, my dad does all that. I looked across the table to the laundry basket that waited for him to collect and bring to the laundry room. He did the laundry and anything else around the house when I was watching TV after dinner. So there the basket sat, just staring at me. I continued across the kitchen to the little red light that indicated the oven was on. I could smell the tart tomatoes and savory cheese in the air while our lasagna was in the long process of cooking in order to be ready for dinner. Something he must have started in my daze when we got home.

I wished I could do the paper on my dad; I could easily thank him for all he does for me and go on and on. I could list the practices and school events he chauffeurs me to, I could write about the millions of nights he had to sit watching some cheesy show or sappy movie instead of what he would prefer.

Then I remembered, the one other time I had strayed from the guidelines instructed by a teacher.

Just a few years ago we were supposed to write a poem about our mothers, but I didn't have enough material. I opted to write about my father. The night before we argued about chores around the house since they had now grown and ate into my free time more that I liked. So I cut a corner and lied to him, saying they were all done. Knowing full well that my bathroom was dirty and the vacuum hadn't been turned on all week.

After he caught me we fought and doors were slammed. By the next morning, we were both remorseful and apologized. So when my class broke into individual projects and we were each told to write a poem about our mothers, I strayed.

I wrote about my father, I knew him inside and out. I knew he took over being both parents, so I thought it fell within the parameters.

When we took turns reading to the class, my teacher pried. After nine months of having me in her class she interjected, "What happened to your mom? Oh honey, how old were you? Oh honey, that must have been terrible..."

Her questions and comments caught me so off guard, I ended up crying in front of the whole class. I ran out of the room and down the hall to the nurse. I didn't ask for permission or anything. I remember the nurse kept asking what hurt and what happened? By the end of it, my dad had to come pick me up and neither one of us wanted to talk about the events that led to my tears.

When it came to my mom any conversations were controlled and my dad's words were measured. The whole thing had a time limit too. We both could only handle so much before it overwhelmed us. That's the unfortunate thing with genetics, we were cut from the same cloth when it came to our emotions.

I turned back to my blank page, ripping myself from my memory of my failed poem from a few years ago.

I stared at it for a long moment before remembering a technique to writing we had learned recently. I started the sentence without knowing where it would take me. I put my pen to the paper and slowly drew out the letters.

My mom.

That's all I got out before I hit that same wall. I closed my eyes scrolling through my memories with her. Most of what I remember is when she was sick, unfortunately. I was too young before then and the memories weren't as close to the surface. The ones that I did have I still do not know for sure if they were memories or just photos and stories told by someone to me. I had a handful that were more vivid, but they were only fragments. I remember riding a carousel with her and my dad, baking in the kitchen, playing in the yard, opening gifts, shopping, traveling to see family, and a bunch of other clips of time. But each memory was blurry and was only a snippet of the full picture.

As I searched the fragments of my mother in my head I felt a jab. She didn't do anything, some of those times she was already starting to get sick. *What had my mother done for me?* I thought, feeling defeated. I felt angered suddenly when the word nothing floated into my head. A pang of embarrassment for myself ran through me.

I raised my pen to the paper again trying to refocus my thoughts. I started the sentence before moving the pen to write my thoughts.

My mom left me.

My mom left me was all I wrote on the page. I read my realization and tears rushed down my cheeks.

"She left me," I let myself say aloud. When the words hit my ears I started to cry hard at our kitchen table. I realized I was sitting out in the open at the table so I wiped at my tears on my cheeks to not alert my father if he came back to check on me. The room was clouded by my tears in my eyes before it flashed and spun.

With this small warning, I wasn't sitting at our kitchen counter; I was in some hospital room with bright light bouncing off the clean white walls. I was staring down at my mother's feet.

"I don't care," she shouted at the doctor and my dad who were both standing just beyond the foot of her bed.

"Rosie, do you hear what he is saying? It isn't safe," my dad said pleading with her.

"I know this is difficult," the doctor started.

"I still don't care. You can't take her from me," my mom said.

I just knew she must be talking about me. I felt my mother's heart pull at the word 'her'. I could feel her longing and tears began gushing from her eyes.

"No one is taking her from you," the doctor began "She can come as often as you want her to. We will extend your visiting hours. You can see your daughter whenever you want."

The word daughter stung when she heard it. She recoiled and swallowed hard.

"I am not doing that to *my* daughter," she said reminding the doctor he had no right to talk about me without her permission. "I don't want her to be scared of hospitals, or have to travel every day, or catch all the diseases in the hallway," she listed pointing to each finger on her hands counting her reasons.

The doctor read her annoyance and waved his hands trying to slow her down. "You won't be in that section of the hospital, she won't be wandering through the main lobby to get to you."

She waved it off "I'm going home," she said with finality. "I want to be with her for as long as I can." When the words left her mouth there was a gut-wrenching pain that took over her body. Every cell hurt and the twist in her throat threatened to take away her voice. "I need to be with her," she squeezed out before letting the pinch in her voice take over.

Her body contorted, her legs squeezed into her chest. Tears clouded the room, I saw my dad hurry around the corner of the bed to console her. He held her upper body and shook trying to hold his own tears back. "I need her," she whispered to him holding tears in with her eyes closed tight.

"We can see what we can do," the doctor started defeated. "But being home carries a lot more risks and expenses. You need to be aware of that."

Without moving her curled form she nodded, accepting his concern.

"We can start the paperwork and see about getting the machines in your home, but you will need to make the space so if you want to talk to Patricia again," he nodded to my dad who was still shaking holding my mother. "She can get you the specifications on what you will need set up in your home. Again, this will be very expensive between the power running in your home, the renting of machines, qualified nurse, and transportation. And you always have the option to come back here if this doesn't work out." He added.

My mother shook her head with urgency, denying this option to be a possibility.

The doctor waved for my dad to follow him. My dad leaned down and kissed her hair before he followed behind the doctor.

My mother watched from the corner of her eye and both men left the room.

Once she knew she was alone she turned over and pulled a stack of papers and photographs from the side table. The photos were warped and the papers were wavy and worn. She took the stack and placed it in front of her face. I saw the first photo; it was a picture of me smiling at the camera with a spoon and what looked like melted ice cream on it. The rim of my mouth was covered in the creamy sweet. She kissed her two fingers and placed them on my cheek before stroking my small face on the glossy paper. She turned to the next photo, another photo of me sitting in a pile of books squeezing a small stuffed orange bear. She pressed the photo to her cheek hugging it into her. When she pulled away I saw the wetness on the photograph from her tear-stained cheek. I now understood the reason the stack had so many warped photos. She flipped to the next photo that was a roughly cut piece of paper that showed my face smiling next to a paper that read, 'I miss you, Mommy'. This was obviously more recent than the previous photos.

"I miss you sweetie, but I'm coming home," she whispered to the worn paper.

She was pulled from her photos when my father and an older familiar nurse entered the room.

"Mrs. Peterson, I just need you to understand a few major points before we can start this process," she started, waiting for my mother to agree to listen.

My mom lifted her body up to a sitting position careful to move around the IV and wires. She placed the stack of pictures in her lap.

"Now, we understand your wish to go home, but outside of the expenses, there are many risks. Without immediate care and response, something that would be easily treatable here might not be from your home. Being around your family may introduce diseases we could have separated you from here. And this may quicken your prognosis," she said aware of what she was telling the couple who stared at her.

"You may end up having less time because you want more time with her," the woman said putting her hands together. "Now I get it, I'm a mom," she swallowed and she moved closer to my mother's bed. "I would do the same thing as you." When she said this she put her hand on my mother's leg affirming her decision. "But I do need you to know, this isn't the optimal choice for your health."

I watched my mother look back to the photo of me holding the sign in her hands.

"I need her to see me as much as she can then." She didn't look to the nurse; she stared at the faded printed photo and let tears flow from her eyes. "If I can't be there with her years from now, I need to be there with her now," she explained the first half of her thought now. Her eyes did not leave my face. The nurse and my dad continued to talk about the logistics and he took notes on the many things he would need to prepare and research in the next few weeks to get my mother moved into our home.

As he nodded and jotted down the instructions, my mother studied him. In between notes, he glanced at her and she mouthed 'thank you' to him. He nodded with a weak smile before writing down the next item the nurse had rattled off.

I was pulled back from this moment with my parents and returned to our kitchen table. I wiped the tears from my eyes that had carried from the memory. I never knew that her being in the house was a disadvantage to her health. I was always a little upset I lost my playroom since the living room limited my space and a lot of my larger toys were squeezed into my room or tucked away. I couldn't quite remember the move-in when she came home but I remember the nurse that had instructed them, she was with us to the end. I remember her meeting me and saying she brought my mother home. I also remembered her hugging me for a long moment at my mother's funeral. My memories blended with hers and I recalled the time in our house. It was less than a year between when she came home and when she had passed.

She didn't leave me, I thought re-reading my paper. I ripped the page from my book careful to not leave a shred of the tainted paper in my workbook. I balled up the offensive page and threw it to the far end of the table. *She did the opposite of leaving me,* I thought. *She gave up everything she had left to be able to be closer to me.*

I turned back to my fresh paper.

My mom would do anything for me.

I started letting the rest flow on the page. I could feel the tears streaking down my eyes, I wrote about my mom and what she did to be near me for that short period. I felt proud to share this with my teacher. Proud to share just how much my mother loved me.

Chapter Seven

LOST NECKLACE

"No, No, No!" I shouted fumbling through my gym bag from school. "I shouldn't have taken it off," I said to myself dumping the remaining items onto the floor. I felt my heart sink when I shuffled through the small pile and didn't see that familiar silver chain in the mix. I continued to push dirty clothes, spare socks, and deodorant around my bedroom floor. I felt the panic set into my stomach.

My dad pushed the door open, "How long does it take to get me your dirty clothes?" He asked looking down at my pile of clothes, bag, and deodorant.

"I lost it," I shouted back. I felt myself begin to cry.

He looked at me confused before walking further into my room. He examined me and my sad pile. "Lost what?" he asked watching me continue to lift and shake out clothes before throwing them back on the floor and starting with the next item.

I didn't even answer him. "I told that stupid gym teacher I didn't need to take it off. And he sent me back to the locker room and said to not come back with it on," I started to sob and kicked the small gym bag away from me.

"What did you lose?" he pressed again starting to collect the items in front of me.

"Mom's necklace," I shouted back "And I should have just left it on, it's never come off and we were just playing badminton. But he's such a jerk he sent me back and said there's no jewelry allowed, school rules." I put my hand to my naked neck, hating that I ever removed the necklace.

My dad didn't respond he just sat close to me on the floor and studied the clothes in his arms.

"I wore that necklace for two weeks at summer camp, on a trampoline, and in the lake and it was fine." I hunched my back thinking of how that's all I had of hers. I felt my dad's hand rubbing my back before he finally reacted.

"Where did you put it?"

"In my locker," I said much louder than was necessary, my head was tilted and tears were escaping through my nose so my voice sounded much more nasal and wet than usual.

"Could it still be there?" he asked trying to brush my hair back to see my face.

"Who knows, we don't have assigned lockers and I'm second period," I said thinking of someone else finding it and keeping my mother's necklace. My body shuddered at the thought.

"Let's go see," he suggested peering below my hair at my wet face. He tried to wipe my tears with his view obstructed from my hair that continued to drown my face. I sniffed hard and coughed choking on the tears in my throat.

"Come on, you never know," he said standing up next to me. "You have to come, they aren't going to let me just wander into the girl's locker room," he reasoned with a joking smile. I could feel him trying to cheer me up but I was too far gone.

"We can't go now," I argued looking up at him. "School's closed," I reminded him.

"Eh, there's always something going on, come on let's go get your necklace," he said so convinced that this was going to be a success.

I stood up and followed him already mourning for my lost gift. I only went along with his plan to give myself time to grieve.

Our house wasn't far from the school and when we turned in sure enough there were about fifty cars in the lot. He always likes to save the day and will drop anything to swoop in and be my hero. So I could feel his faith in himself when we drove to the school and it practically reverberated in the small space of the car circling the crowded lot. He parked in the closest open spot and we could hear music coming from the auditorium.

"There's a play," I explained, "Anastasia I think." I felt some relief at knowing we could at least get near the locker room, just hoping this would work out the way my hopeful father had envisioned in his head.

We walking in together and made our way to the gymnasium while he waved to the obviously unlocked building as if he did a magic trick.

As we passed the auditorium he asked "Why don't you ever try out for the plays?"

"Dad" I grumbled back. "I can barely survive presentations in class never mind a whole audience of people," I explained spotting Chrissy, the girl a grade above me standing in the middle of the stage twirling. A small dog followed her on the stage while she sang skipping and raising her arms. I felt myself sigh and looked away, I did wish I had the confidence. Chrissy was usually the star and always talked about how much fun these plays were.

"Your mother used to love to perform, especially sing. Once you were born, you were her favorite audience though. She would hold you close and sing every song she's ever known." He finished his thought then I heard him suck in and hold his breath.

It always kind of shocked me when he would mention her, it was usually small tidbits. So far I've learned she didn't like the corners on brownies, couponing, visors, expensive sunglasses (according to my dad she almost always broke or lost them immediately), and now I know she loved to sing and perform.

When my dad would mention these little facts it was usually not a long conversation or story just a quick tagline with some random piece of information about her. I kept a personal catalog in my head. We had a lot in common, except for how much she loved the rain. She loved the sound and feeling of water when it hit her. I loved the sunshine and the rain just made me want to snuggle with soup and a movie. Now I can add performing for a crowd, another difference we had.

We finally made it to the gym. I paused before turning the handle waiting for it to fight back, like it usually did if you tried to use the gym outside of your class time. Even if it was your period for gym, you had to wait for a gym teacher to unlock it. For some reason today it wasn't locked. I about fell over finding this door unlocked. Now I was starting to believe that my dad really did perform magic, although he did not hold this door open like it was another trick. We went through the doors and were met with complete silence. These heavy doors completely shut out the singing and the audience's applause. I turned toward the girl's locker room.

"I'll wait here," my dad announced stopping along the wall. He fell into the padding and waited.

I opened the girl's locker room door, again shocked when the door did not protest back. I couldn't believe how far we had succeeded at this point. I entered the locker room, the sensor lights kicked on and lit the rows of lockers.

I made my way to my usual locker. Although we didn't have assigned lockers, there was a spot in the corner that I preferred. Closest to the mirrors, with the bench not blocking the path, and it was furthest from the door. I opened the one I remember using earlier that day and stood up on my toes to see the contents of the top shelf. A small glimmer caught my eye and I felt my heart explode. It's here, it's still here. I grabbed the necklace and returned it to my neck rushing to close the clasp landing it safe and sound in its rightful home. I stood there smiling; almost hugging it in my hands I was so happy I didn't lose this one piece of my mom forever.

A sudden flash and I was no longer in the girl's locker room. I was outside, somewhere unfamiliar. I was on the edge of grass that stood above the rest of the yard. I looked down the small slope in front of me at six smiling faces; I could hear myself singing to them.

It came back to me, my experience in camp and the hospital. I'm not me; I'm my mom right now. I caught sight of my jeans and green top, definitely not me. I don't own anything that looks like what my body is currently wearing. I felt my arms stretch out then hug my body close. I listened while my mom sang. One song closed, she would bow and listen while the small group applauded then she would straighten up and start into a new song. I could hear her voice resonate in her head it was somehow familiar. I could just barely recognize her voice from a distant memory. I searched my mind for the memory while I continued to listen to her sing. Her small audience grew. People arrived and came to greet her before settling in to her audience. She continued to sing song after song.

I could feel the release of each note from her body. It was a sweet satisfying rush that grew for the longer notes. When she would draw her stomach in and let the wind flow through into her lungs. A slight vibration in her throat would shake the note before the rush of air was pushed out. I relished in her feeling of completeness and pride with each song. Somehow my singing in the shower couldn't come close to this amazing feeling of grace and control right now.

I felt her eyes follow a woman from the house to the left of where she stood. The woman was wearing an apron and waving her hands.

"Come on sweetie, it's time," she shouted to my mom and the small audience. They all applauded one last time and each started to share their love and appreciation for her voice. I listened to her thank them all and tell the crowd about when she would be performing in the talent show. The whole group walked together. I studied the house they were approaching and felt another twang of a memory. My grandparents' house? I kind of remember it from pictures at my grandpa's condo where he lived after. My mom led the group and opened the door to this familiar house. She continued to talk about songs and performances with her audience. These appeared to be other family members. I heard her say Aunt and Uncle here and there. The group of family members followed her into the house and disbursed to say hi to a small group of women that helped the woman in the apron. I saw the familiar eyes on this woman's face; my grandma was hurrying around the kitchen and welcoming our group into the house.

I watched my grandma nod to a familiar-looking man standing in the corner of the kitchen, my grandpa. He pulled a string that hung above his shoulder and a small banner unrolled over the far counter. It read 'HAPPY BIRTHDAY ROSIE!' with a small rose painted after the exclamation point.

"Happy Birthday" they all cried in unison then they began to sing Happy Birthday to her. They sang and my grandparents met to stand arm in arm under the small banner. My grandma held the last note and covered my grandpa's mouth. He had started the song to guess my mom's age but she was stifling his solo and my mom laughed. It was fun to see my grandparents like this so active and young. They were so excited and happy while singing happy birthday. My mom continued to giggle at her father until he had given up his struggle to get his song out. My grandma then picked up the cake that was tucked behind where they stood. She closed the space between herself and my mom and held the cake up with its flickering candles. My mom blew out the candles in the center of the plain white cake with green sprinkles dancing along the edges. After the candles went out they all cheered and started to hug my mom.

My mom helped my grandma cut the cake and disburse the pieces before grabbing her piece, a larger corner slice, and collecting her fork from the pile on the counter.

One of the less familiar faces in the crowd crept in beside me with their piece of cake. "Are you going to grow up to be a singer?" she asked putting a forkful of cake into her mouth and smiling at my mom.

I felt my mom look down at her cake and shake her head. "No, I just do it for fun. I love the feeling I get when I sing. Maybe I can grow up to teach others to sing though." she responded backing away from the counter to make her way to the couch. She finished the piece of cake next to my great uncle. I had started to recognize about half the people in the room now while they all settled in and enjoyed their slices. I listened to her uncle entertain the crowd with stories of when they dropped the whole cake for their son. Everyone laughed while he continued with the story explaining that they improvised with candles in donuts that they had bought earlier that day.

His son sat near the doorway to the next room and asked "Can we have donuts too?" before he abandoned his slice of cake on the table and came running over.

"I think we created a monster," my great uncle joked and everyone laughed in unison. When I saw the small boy come closer I recognized my second cousin, much younger than I have ever seen him. He now works in the city and we see him at major family events. I watched him stomp his way back to the slice of cake and finish with his back to his dad in a sign of protest.

My mom stood up and collected the empty plates from those that were sitting in the small circle with her. She turned into the kitchen but my grandma stopped her and grabbed the plates.

"My gift is the small white box wrapped with the green ribbon," she told my mom gesturing to the table with gifts spread out.

My mom's body made its way to the table and collected the small gift that matched this description. Everyone remained in the other room finishing their cake and adding sugar and cream to their coffees. I could hear laughing, her uncle finished another story. I thought of family events now in my life, he still is the entertainment, just a little older now.

My mom walked back and met my grandma by the open dishwasher.

"I can't wait anymore, open it now," my grandma instructed wiping her wet hands on her apron and kicking the dishwasher closed.

I felt two strong hands land on my shoulders and my grandpa said "Happy birthday sweetheart" to my mom before joining my grandma by the dishwasher and smiling at her.

My mom looked down at the small box; she untied the bow and lifted the lid. Inside hung a small silver heart from a chain. The heart looked as though it was created with bundles of sticks that were bent into the shape of a heart. The two arches of the bundles came down to meet a small knot that held them into a point. I recognized this necklace, the very necklace she left to me. I could feel my mind reel feeling guilty for almost losing this precious gift. My mom ran her fingers down the shape of the heart and my grandma interrupted her.

"So you can always sing to the trees," my grandma told her. My mom looked up to meet her eyes.

I felt my mom's eyes narrow and she cocked her head in confusion.

"That was your first audience you know," my grandpa continued and my grandma nodded "you used to go outside and sing into the woods. You would tell us the branches moving in the wind were the tree's way of applauding for you," he smiled finishing his explanation.

"I do remember that! I love it!" She shouted starting to remove the necklace from the box and unhitch the small circle clasp. She pulled the necklace under her hair before closing the clasp on the base of her neck. I felt her heart swell in her chest and she looked at both my grandparents "Thank you! I really love it! I'll never take it off."

"It looks beautiful, just like you," my grandma said diving in to hug my mom. "Happy birthday my amazing girl, now the trees will always hear you" she continued leaning away to look at my mom's face.

My grandpa reached in for a hug and we heard someone announce. "Smile," from behind us. We turned in unison and saw a less familiar face holding a small silver camera aimed at us. The flash was blinding since we were all taken off guard. The impromptu photographer laughed at the result of our blindsided photo and then aimed the camera at us once more saying, "Attempt two."

My grandma put her arm around my mom's back and my grandpa reached across until my mom was sandwiched between the two of them. My mom smiled and waited for the flash. The flash went off blinding me for a second. I blinked the light out of my eyes and arrived back in the locker room.

I felt myself regain control of my arms and I rubbed my thumb on that familiar bottom edge of the heart. I smiled, feeling the gift hang on my neck against my skin. Shutting my locker, I thanked my luck that the necklace remained and I didn't lose something that meant so much.

I walked out of the locker room door back into the gym my dad remained in the same spot against the wall.

"Any luck?" he asked making a few slow steps toward me with his eyes searching.

"Yes!" I announced back skipping to him before the two of us started toward the exit.

"See, I told you. No need to worry," he said putting his arm around me. "Next time just tuck it into your shirt so the teacher doesn't see it," He whispered winking at me

"Yeah, I will never take this off again," I responded reaching up and feeling relief that her necklace was hanging at home against my neck. I slowed my pace; I wanted to ask him a question but didn't want to be met by the sounds of the audience and the play when I asked. He reached to pull the door open to leave the gym but I interrupted before he could squeeze the handle.

"Did mom ever teach singing or perform before..." I let myself trail off. We both knew the end of that sentence.

He blinked wildly for a few moments before starting to speak. "Your mom," he paused letting his arm fall and turning to face me. "Your mom always used to sing to you. Before you were born she would help out at plays and teach children here and there. But once she had you..." He searched his memories. "She would walk you to the edge of the woods by our house and sing while you slept or played. Her parents would roll their eyes and say "She's always done this." I am not sure where it came from but her favorite place to sing was under the trees. We would let you two have your time out by the trees since you always seemed calmer from her voice."

He chuckled a little. "Sometimes you wouldn't sleep until you heard her, so she had to sing you to sleep. When she went away for a weekend when you were little I swear you stayed up thirty-six hours in protest," He told me ruffling up my hair.

He saw how intent I was listening and his face got more serious. "She loved the feeling of sharing her voice with others and once she had you," he paused again looking for the words He let a long breath escape before continuing "She wanted to share it with you. Wanted you to sing too, I

77

remember when you were just about a year old we were hanging around on a Saturday and I was down the hall. I heard a soft noise then your mom yelped. Next thing I heard was excited screaming. I came running into the room expecting to see your first steps. She was so excited and we knew it would have been any day now." He laughed shaking his head thinking of this memory. "I came in and both of you were sitting on the floor, your mom was in the happiest tears I had ever seen. I stared waiting for an explanation of what happened that got her so excited. Once she composed herself she said "She sang, she sang to me!' and she kept saying it. I had to laugh." He continued smiling at me "I told her I thought you must have walked or something and she just waved it off, "She sang!" He waved his hand then smiled bright at the two last words, impersonating my mom all those years ago.

"That's all she would talk about. Most people would ask if you were walking or talking yet. Every time she would cut them off, "She can sing!" she would say, so proud. Eventually, you walked and talked but I would bet your mom celebrated your singing ten times more than your first steps." He got a little more serious. "She sang to you every day, until…" he trailed off breaking his eye contact. He left that same silence to finish his sentence.

I felt my smile fade thinking of how she was before. Thinking of her voice, how she was in the memory, and how she sang for me in a time before I could remember.

He picked his eyes back up and saw my somber face. "She loved you so much, sweetie. You were her last student when you were little; she always talked about the rush of singing and how it felt to have others hear her. I know when she heard your little tiny voice that first time, she couldn't wait for you to feel it too."

I searched his face thinking of her excitement and love while she sang for her family. I had blurs of memories of her singing when I was much younger and she wasn't sick, but they were faded and almost dreamlike. I wasn't really sure which were memories and which were created out of missing my mom.

Just as quickly as it started it was over, we were done talking about her. I knew he needed a moment to loose himself in memories. I took this time to store every detail about her in the front of my mind. The catalog of what I knew about her growing that afternoon.

We walked back through the school the way we came in, I heard the familiar song of Anastasia echoing through the lobby. I listened to Chrissy when the song came to a climatic close and the audience cheered. I felt myself look through the small crack in the door and see her standing alone on the stage with her arms up. With the final clang of the band, the lights blinked out on the stage. I saw the silhouettes of the audience as they stood up in small groups that seemed to spread across the floor like a wave. They cheered and clapped and the dim lights came back on denoting intermission. That broke my focus from the stage, I turned back toward our journey out of the school but I saw a small desk by the front office that housed any major events or flyers that the school has decided to share with us. On the closest corner sat a pile of papers that announced 'AUDITIONS' on the top. I felt my body change course and met with the table. I read the piece of paper that was providing the information for the next school play's auditions. I held the paper in one hand and reached up to squeeze the necklace with the other. I thought of my mom singing in the woods when she was my age and again when I was little. I felt the rush of having her voice heard and enjoyed by others. I folded the paper into fourths and shoved it in my back pocket before turning back toward the exit. My dad had stopped walking when I changed course and stood there watching me. I walked toward him and he smiled at me.

"Just in case," I said a little sheepish.

"I think you will be great," he smiled at me and we left the school.

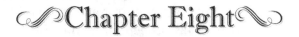Chapter Eight

FIRST DATE

There's nothing. I thought to myself pushing all the hangers in my closet to the right. I began thumbing through my clothes for the third time. At this point, I could feel sweat gathering on my upper lip and at the base of my back. I grabbed the corner of my towel wrapped around my head helping to speed up the process of drying my hair and dabbed my lip. I reached the middle of my closet and I let out a growl at my clothes. *I have nothing.* I thought again staring at my expansive collection of shirts, hoodies, dresses, jeans, and leggings. I was stepping on the first four tops I pulled down from the hanger, laid against my body then threw to the floor in distaste. When I came to the end of the line for the fourth time now I saw a top I somehow missed before. It was a sleeveless shirt with a faded look to it, with both a deep V on the front and back. Not too deep for me to be uncomfortable but enough for me to feel special. I pulled the shirt from my closet and turned back to my mirror holding the fabric against the damp towel still wrapped around me. "Aha," I exclaimed flipping my head over all in one motion and let the towel holding my hair unravel and hit the floor. With that motion I started toward my drawers to grab a bra and underwear. I heard Brownie rise from his usual spot on my bed, cross my room then make three

81

circles before plopping on my clean clothes and the damp towel resting on the floor. I grabbed jeans from my dresser, these were my go-to jeans and again I was going to wear these bad boys. I re-dried my whole body realizing how much I was sweating. The shirt and jeans clung to me briefly when I put them on. I posed in front of my mirror and smiled. I turned to Brownie who was now fast asleep on his favorite bed in the house, my clothes. "How do I look?" I asked him modeling my ensemble and spinning around since he needed the full effect to answer. He didn't lift his head, but he did open his eyes to watch me in my small show. "I thought so too," I responded to him walking over and pulling the damp towel from under his bottom half. He sighed then pulled his legs in tighter over my clothes.

I brought the towels into the bathroom and hung them on their respective hooks before searching for the hairdryer. I think I've used this thing three times in my life but thanks to how long it took to pick out my current outfit, this was a last resort. I dried my hair and applied my one lip gloss. This was one of three items of makeup that I owned, just light pink with gold flecks of glitter dancing in the bottle. I contemplated attempting to use the shadow and mascara that were sitting in the drawer where I pulled the lip gloss from. Holding up the mascara, I braced myself. For some reason the whole act of practically jabbing yourself in the eye made me cringe. My eyes started to water at the memory of brushing my cornea the first time I tried this product. I remembered that burning sensation and leaned in as close to the mirror as I could get then applied one layer of mascara careful to not bring the wand too close to my fragile eye. I leaned back happy to see the end product wasn't a bloodshot eye again and smiled at myself. I applied the mascara to my other eye with the same level of care, before admiring the effect in my reflection. I turned to leave the bathroom and jumped back almost teetering backward onto the bath mat.

"So first date?" my dad asked smiling at me taking in my mascara and slightly more revealing than normal top.

"Yeah," I stammered trying to squeeze by him back to the safety of my room.

"You said you guys were going to see a movie?"

"Yeah," I squeaked out racing down the hallway to my room. I took a mental inventory of what I still had to do. I still had to pull out my babysitting money from my stash in the top drawer of my dresser, pick a bag (which shouldn't take long, I only own two), and put on my shoes. Lucky for me, no decision on shoes needed, when I wore these jeans I always wore my grey shoes. The stitching in the jeans was grey too and I loved the appearance of them in combination.

"You know that was my first date too," my dad continued staying two steps behind me on my rush back to my room.

"Okay," I interjected while I stood in my doorway holding the door and facing him. "Sorry dad I have to finish getting ready" I said shutting the door on his surprised expression.

"Okay Hun," he said after a moment through the closed door. "Just let me know if you need anything."

Once back in my room I checked the time, I still had a few minutes before he said he would be here. He has a car and license but since he just got both he can't be out late so we were seeing an early movie and not doing dinner. The movie fell practically at dinnertime so I debated hiding a granola bar in my small bag. Then thought about how insane I would look whipping out a granola bar in a theater. *Popcorn it is* I thought smiling to myself so I chose the small clutch I got as a gift last Christmas from my Uncle.

I shoved the cash in there and stood contemplating anything else I might need. I debated going back to the bathroom to collect the lip gloss but feared this would spark another awkward conversation with my dad.

I zipped the floppy bag closed. Its only contents were a small wad of money and my cell phone so the fabric barely held its rectangular shape. Then I bent over Brownie who remained sleeping in front of my closet on my clothes and reached for my grey shoes. I finished my outfit and held my prepared bag, noting I still had all of one-minute left. *Perfect* I thought to myself plopping on the edge of my bed waiting to hear a car outside. Luckily we were one of the last houses on a cul-de-sac so not many cars were roaming around. I felt confident there would be no false alarms, so I just sat in silence avoiding my dad.

After five minutes I joined Brownie on the floor petting his head and chest, he rolled over to encourage me to continue. I weighed going out of my room to wait but really wasn't ready for any more questions from my dad.

Another five minutes, I could feel my heart racing. I worried about all the things that could go wrong on this date. I mean I've known him forever and had a crush on him for as long as I could remember, but he's the one who asked me out. Could he be having second thoughts? I felt for my phone in my bag and debated calling him, then worried I might not like the response. I paused on the zipper willing the self-conscious questioning to loosen their grip on my thoughts. I continued to sit on the floor with Brownie and listened for anything outside that would imply he was here. After twenty minutes of spoiling Brownie and feeling my heart race in my chest, I finally heard a car on the driveway. Brownie shot up and ran to my closed door barking. I stood up and let him free so he could continue to bark at the closed front door. I brushed off the loose hair that landed on me and took inventory again. I had my bag, my shoes and I was ready. I felt sick, but I was ready. My dad walked to the door to open it for Brownie then slowed at the car in the driveway. "Looks like he's here," he said turning back to me.

I looked through the sheer curtains and saw a beat up brown car.

With that, I was somewhere else. I watched the new room unfold. I blinked and saw my grandma hunched in front of my face. I took in my new surroundings and realized I was once again in my mother's memories. My mom was smiling and laughing with her mom in a bathroom I've never seen before.

"So tell me about him?" my grandma requested and she applied something to my mom's face. I felt a smile rush across my mom's face before she responded to her mom.

"He's so sweet and funny," my mom said tucking her hair behind her ears. It was much longer now than in the past few memories I traveled back to. "And he said he's been trying to ask me out for months, I thought we were just friends," she continued and my grandma listened intently while putting something else on her face. I felt the soft brush on her cheeks and into her hairline , she closed her eyes and said "When he finally did I felt so excited, I didn't even think of him that way but as he stood there shy and vulnerable I felt a shift inside." She opened her eyes and pointed to a light pink tube. "That one." She waited and my grandma applied some gloss to her lips. I could feel her wriggle in the chair with excitement, she was fidgeting everywhere from the neck down and her hands were spinning in her lap. Her mom had to compensate for the moving target so leaned in close to get the perfect curve of her upper lip.

"He's the one you have been telling me about? You always partner with him in gym?"

"Yeah," she answered dancing in her seat, before pressing her lips together and making a smacking noise a few times. "He's always making me laugh so we usually stay on the same team and joke around all through gym."

"Perfect," my grandma told my mom backing away so my mom could look in the mirror.

"Thanks, Mom," my mom said before hugging her and turning to race out of the room.

"Let me know if you need anything else," I heard my grandma call out to her when she jogged into her room. Her room was simple with pictures of friends circling the walls. She had her bed almost the same way I did, against the far wall closest to the window. A small pile of stuffed animals against the wall on the bed. In front of the closet sat a small pile of clothes that she scooped up and threw on the green chair to the right of the closet. She went over to her dresser and sprayed a small pink bottle that smelled like sweet flowers into the air. She watched the mist glitter in the light before fading in front of her and she walked through it. Almost like she just cast a spell. Again she angled the bottle behind her and sprayed into the air then took a step back walking through the second cloud of scent. She put the bottle on the dresser then grabbed a small purse sitting next to it. When she grabbed the bag she heard the doorbell. Her eyes shot to the clock on the other end of the dresser, 7:25 the clock read. "He's early," she whispered to herself. She turned to the mirror and smiled at her own face before looking down at her outfit. She wore a simple black top with a small V-neck showcasing the parallel lines between her shirt and the heart necklace we shared. She looked at the necklace reaching up to straighten the heart then took the clasp that was resting on her collarbone and rotated it up to the base of her neck. She smiled one more time at herself then dashed out of the room. Turning the corner, she listened to her mom laughing and speaking to her date until she entered the room. When she approached, I studied the date's face. The edges were familiar to me somehow, I tried to place the profile to my memories but couldn't quite pin down where I had seen him before.

My mom joined the group consisting of my grandma, grandpa, and her date and stood there shoulder to shoulder with him.

"What did I miss?" she asked looking at her date.

Once his face met hers I saw his eyes. *Dad?* I thought while my mom's memory continued to play out in front of me. I recognized those eyes, I know those eyes all too well. I didn't hear what they were saying. I was lost in my own mind. Her first date was with Dad? How did no one ever tell me this? I knew that they were together for a long time but I had no idea this is when it started. I reeled back and started to pay attention, my grandparents wished her well. When my grandma hugged my mom tight she whispered "You're right he is funny." She peeled away from the hug and beamed at my dad. "It was nice to meet you Leo." The two of them smiled at each other before my mom turned and walked out with my dad toward a small sedan sitting in the driveway.

I could hear the dull voices of my grandparents in the house behind them. My mom turned back for a second and saw them both standing at the window by the door. They watched my mom and dad walk to the car. My grandma was holding a small black object in front of her chest. When my mom saw it she turned back around and I saw the whole neighborhood twirl. She rolled her eyes at whatever her parents were up to then turned back to my dad.

"The paparazzi are on the clock behind us," she warned.

My dad turned to face her house and laughed. "My mom would have done the same thing at my house," he waved to the house and started to make poses and large fake smiles.

My mom laughed watching him pose for the camera before pulling his arm down from the air "Don't encourage them, I won't be surprised if they show up at the movies," she warned him.

"So that's why they asked the theater, movie, and time," he replied stroking his chin as if he was solving a mystery. "Eh, let them come. The theater would never let them in with a camera thanks to all those movie pirates out there," he said shrugging.

"I guess," my mom said turning to see her parents smiling back and waving. The flash went off again on the camera aimed at my mom and dad.

"You have no idea the deal I had to make with my brother to borrow this car," he said skipping in front of my mom to open her door for her.

"Do I even want to know?" my mom playfully asked before slipping into the car. He closed the door behind her and walked around the car smiling. He opened his door and fell into his seat.

"Well for one I had to clean it, but I think I would have had to do that either way," he said motioning to the dark spots on the dashboard left by the sun's damage being blocked by multiple items in a wide variety of sizes and shapes. "You wouldn't believe how much garbage was sitting up there. But other than that, yeah you don't want to know" he winked at her. He started the engine and pulled out of the driveway.

They laughed and smiled at each other the whole drive to the movies. Touching on an inside joke from their gym class together about a boy named Edwin who had his fourth broken bone of the year already. They joked about how hard my mom snorted the first time he made her laugh in gym, and she laughed harder when he started telling her stories of the crazy things he discovered in the car before going to pick her up.

My dad parked and the two of them walked into the theater. Halfway to the theater, another car turned down their row. The car approached at a reasonable rate but my dad closed the distance and called out "I'll protect you." He put one arm over my mom's shoulder to complete his joke. He looked down at her face. I felt the warmth of the blood flushing her cheeks.

"I really just wanted to have an excuse to get close to you," he said winking at her. He lowered his arm and grabbed for my mom's hand. I felt her smile and meet eyes with him again.

He dropped her hand at the doors and pulled them open for her to enter. When they joined the ticket line he replaced his hand. It felt as if it had cooled in the brief period where he was not holding my mom's hand. Once replaced my mom's whole arm was heating up with this gesture. They stood side by side in line and talked about their synopses on the other movies playing and what they've heard. They laughed about what they knew of the comedy they were going to see and pointed to the movie poster hung high behind the counter. With that, I recognized the movie. It was obviously old by the time I heard about it and I have seen it playing on television before. I had watched with friends, it was a hilarious, quirky comedy that could never go out of style. I thought back to when it would play on weekends or if I would discover it on while sick at home, my dad would always leave the room. Usually, since it was just the two of us I got to pick movies and TV, he watched his sports and action movies late at night or when I was at school events and friend's houses. But on a few occasions, I had seen this movie playing on TV and flipped it on. He would always find an excuse and busy himself with a project out of the line of sight of the TV in our living room. I felt guilty for forcing this movie on my dad not knowing the memory tied to it.

I looked through my mom's eyes watching him smile at her continuing to impersonate the main character from the movie trailer. The two of them laughed and kept holding up the line not aware of the moving patrons in front of them. The space would grow until someone deeper behind them in line would gesture to the opening they had left. They were both so happy in this memory it was no wonder the movie was hard for him to see now. The guilt rose, I recollected the many times I quoted the film just like they were now.

I was pulled by my own thoughts when they were called to be next at the register. My dad kept a firm grasp on my mom's hand and he pulled her to the register. He requested the two tickets and joked that they were at the kid's rate. The man behind the counter did not seem to be entertained by my dad's joke. He handed the cash to the stoic faced employee then collected the printed tickets and put them in his pocket before rushing to return his hand to my mom's.

The two walked to the concession stand. "Okay now don't judge me," my dad said turning to my mom with a very serious look on his face "But I love movie theater snacks. I don't know why, maybe it's the stale popcorn they store in garbage bags or the fact that they price everything at three times its actual value. But this is… usually my favorite part of the movies." He turned and pointed toward the options of candy. "I'm going to get the Reese's Pieces, popcorn, a cherry slushie and for dessert, chocolate covered cookie dough. What can I get for you?" he asked. The line shortened and they both took a step forward.

"I always get the blue raspberry slushie and Twizzlers," my mom replied motioning toward the only other slushie option.

"Awesome, so we won't have to fight 'till the death for any of my food?" my dad joked.

"I didn't say anything about not stealing your popcorn," she replied squinting at him putting on a tough face. Her eyes were soft around the grimace playing with my dad.

"Fair enough, I'll just get the biggest one they have. What's that one called again, the trough?" he joked and my mom laughed. It was fun to see my dad this way, so light-hearted and almost silly.

The two ordered and collected their goodies from the counter. He gathered the majority of the items, shoving the candy boxes into his pockets and only leaving the blue slushie for my mom to hold with her free hand.

"Theater three," my dad noted leading the way into the theater. He balanced the pile of goodies and fished for the ticket before they could go in. I watched him carefully keep everything balanced and one elbow available to push the door open for my mom to enter the theater.

As the two paused at the back of the theater, he motioned for her to pick a spot.

"Wherever you want Rosie," he said staying just behind her. She shuffled toward the middle row then the middle seat. He followed suit and the two sat down then spread out the snacks and drinks. Others filled in the spaces around them while they continued to laugh and munch on their snacks, unaware that anyone else was even in the room. They shared the popcorn and my mom leaned in closer each time she reached for a handful. The lights started to fade and a green screen with the white text advertising the rating of the preview that was about to play. My mom turned and whispered.

"So why is the food and candy only... usually your favorite part of the movies?" she asked eying my dad lit up only by the trailer that had begun to play on the screen.

He smiled "Because this time you're my favorite part," he whispered back before leaning toward my mom. He kissed her on the cheek, I could feel her whole body heat up and her heart beat faster in her chest. If it weren't for gravity, she might float right out of the chair. He piled all the goodies and popcorn in the empty chair next to him then leaned into my mom putting one arm around her shoulders.

I was brought back to my living room, looking out the window at the brown car. "You better tell him to come in here and meet your old man," my dad said to me in a much deeper voice than usual. I looked up and saw his aged face and fading hair, nothing like what I had just seen earlier on their first date. I was half-aware of my shocked expression studying his face. How it had changed from my mother's memory. I shook my head and I brought my mind back to the present. The two of us turned to face the car again. I saw no movement coming from the driver seat though.

I could feel my anticipation growing, waiting for him to come to the door but embarrassed that he still had not. I thought back to the memory of my dad and mom's first date and felt myself react to protect my own embarrassment, "Times have changed Dad, it's not like when you and Mom were our age," I said. His head bobbed back, looking like he was just punched in the face. Immediately I regretted my words, but I could feel my defenses building to protect myself from his judgment.

He looked out at the car again. The pile of clothes almost blocking the rearview window, the light coating of pollen on the whole car tinting it a yellow-green, and a collection of bumper stickers that were insulting to any car close enough to read them. I watched my dad's face contort with what I could only assume to be his own remembrance of their first date. His body tensed up and I could hear his breath catch. "What time is that movie?" he asked continuing to stare out the window.

"Starts in twenty," I said realizing he was looking to escape from the memory of his first date and how much he still missed my mom.

He turned and hugged me, "Have fun," he said "and don't stay out too late."

"We will be right back after the movie, Dad," I replied reaching for the door. I escaped not just from my protective dad but from my words that still hung in the air. 'You and Mom' continued to echo in my ears begging to be taken back. Now that I was outside I was able to drown out my words with the pounding music I could hear coming from his car.

I walked to the car, the music was louder with each step. He sat in the front seat feverishly texting someone.

I knocked on the window to draw his attention and he barely looked up from his phone before shouting "It's open," over the deafening music.

Sure enough it was unlocked, so I opened the door and sank into the car.

"Where were you? I texted like fifty times. We are going to be late," he continued to shout over the music. I looked at the radio waiting for him to lower the volume or turn the unfamiliar hateful sounding music off. He continued to stare at me turning his phone toward my face.

"Can we turn it down or something?" I shouted pointing at the volume knob.

"Fine," he said lowering the volume and putting his phone in a trash-filled cup holder by the stick shift. I followed the phone down and looked around the trash-filled car. I noticed the stale odor that was taking over the small space. I had to open the window a few inches to let in some less nauseating smelling air. When I reached for the seatbelt I saw piles of garbage invading my seat from the back. There were tissues, food bags, empty envelopes crumpled into balls, and wrappers for some kind of protein bar that boys seem to be obsessed with.

"So," he continued, "Did you lose my number or something?" He asked annoyed slamming the car into first and propelling us out of my driveway.

"No I have it, I just didn't hear it in my bag," I said holding up the small bag.

"Whatever, we might be able to make it," he said changing gears with an awkward jolt while the engine protested painfully. He took a tight turn and I heard various items jumble around his backseat, plastic bags rustled in the wind from my open window. He put the music back up and I tried to meet his eye, this was too loud and the music was so dark. He kept his eyes trained on the road and continued to jab into each change of gears on our way to the theater. I opened the window more and tried to keep my eyes fixed forward, his horrible timing on the gear change created jerky transitions that were starting to make me feel sick.

We pulled into the theater and he sped into a spot at an awkward angle with the back bumper on my side almost meeting the car next to us. I squeezed out of my door careful not to damage his filthy car or hurt the neighboring car. I turned to meet him in the road but I saw just how small a space between his trunk and the car he parked next to. *I'll never fit through that,* I thought turning to walk around the car.

When I reached his side and I looked up to see he was already three cars away, "Come on we are going to miss it," he shouted back to me making his way toward the theater.

Wasn't he the one late? I thought, speeding up to try to close the distance between us.

"The movie shouldn't be starting for another ten minutes," I noted once I was only a few steps behind him.

"No, it started five minutes ago," he argued walking even faster. I searched my memory for what I had read online only earlier that day. How did I get the times mixed up?

He pulled the door open for himself and sped through it, I caught the door and it almost took me with it. He rushed inside unaware of my small battle with the heavy door. Now that we were both inside I caught up to him and we got in line behind the few people already waiting. He continued to jump around and pace in the small space of the line. I looked up at the movie and the times offered then read the clock just above.

"See we have like ten minutes," I explained pointing to the times.

"We aren't seeing that movie. I saw it already and it's not good enough to see again." He pointed to the black and red poster depicting the gory movie I had avoided even seeing the trailer to. "We are seeing that movie," he said.

I stared at the poster then noted the times. Sure enough it started six minutes ago now. "I thought we agreed to see that new comedy," I said.

"Yeah but I ended up seeing it last night so I don't want to pay to see the same movie. Besides it wasn't even that good."

I thought back to our conversation on Wednesday where we agreed to see this movie. Friday, before we left school we agreed on the time. We don't usually talk on the phone or text so I hadn't talked to him since then. I still haven't opened my phone to clear those 'fifty' messages he claims to have sent me earlier. I was lost in thought when we were called to be next. I followed him to the register but was shocked when he turned to face me.

"What are you doing? It will be faster if you get your own register," he shouted into my face. I was jolted back from his demand and stepped back into line by walking backward to avoid making eye contact with the other patrons for any further embarrassment. After we each bought our tickets I joined him by the end of the registers. "What did you want to get for snacks?" I asked starting toward the concession stand.

"We have to go to nine, that's all the way over here. Plus there's no time," he responded reading his ticket and making his way toward theaters nine to fifteen. I followed behind him and I felt my mouth water with the smell of butter and popcorn. I really regretted not packing that granola now. After handing over our tickets he darted into the theater that was almost pitch black. I lost him the second we walked in while my eyes attempted to adjust to the darkness.

"What are you doing?" I heard him say from a few steps up the row behind me, I searched the darkness for any form of a person. Finally, something lit up the screen and I had a few seconds of light to follow him up. He walked without talking to me to the back row against the wall in the far corner. *I have never sat this far from the screen in my life,* I thought.

I joined in the seat next to him, "Can't we go a little closer?" I asked motioning to the dozen or so of empty rows of seats in front of us before the next closest person.

"This is where I always sit," he argued back. He waved down the aisle to a boy from our school that also appeared to be on a date. The low light making it difficult to find his face in the dark. I settled for looking at the area where I heard his voice emanating from, assuming this to be his face.

About ten minutes into the movie my stomach started to growl so loud I was convinced it would disrupt the other movie-goers. I wanted so bad to sneak out of the theater just for some popcorn. I looked over at him and he was intently watching the movie. I sat there bored and hungry until one particularly gruesome scene turned my stomach. Silver lining, I guess I'm not hungry anymore.

At the end of the movie, I was sick to my stomach and annoyed. I had paid my own hard-earned money to see this movie. He stood up almost tripping over me while I sat there questioning how all this happened.

"Are you asleep down there?" he asked motioning to the other patrons who were starting to rise and exit the theater.

I wish, I thought straightening my stiff body. How long was that movie? I peeked at my phone in my bag, almost three hours. How did I not fall asleep? I felt the blood return to my legs and we walked out of the theater.

"That movie was awesome right?" He asked pulling out his phone. I didn't answer. Nothing I said would have reinforced his rhetorical question. He began to text someone while we walked with the small crowd to the exit. "Oh hold on, I gotta piss," he announced when we approached the bathrooms. I turned to say meet you out here but he had already cut the corner and disappeared.

I walked in and washed what remained of the lip gloss and mascara off my face. This was by far the worst 3 hours, not to mention worst date. I contemplated hiding in the bathroom and calling my dad to pick me up. I didn't want to climb back in his horrible car for another jerky ride while continuing to permanently damage my eardrums. I felt too embarrassed to call my dad and hide in here so I finally decided to go back out and just get this thing over with. When I got out of the bathroom he stood against the wall with his face in his phone again.

"I was wondering where you ran off to." he said keeping his eyes fixed on his phone. "Are you ready yet?" he asked "If I'm not home by nine, I lose car privileges," he explained starting toward his car not even waiting for my response.

Once we got back to his car I was relieved to see the neighboring car had left so I wouldn't have to complete that long walk and squeeze into the door again. I fell into the car and was greeted with that same stale smell.

Buckled in now I was thankful I didn't get to eat. Again I was bounced around in the blaring music while he attempted to drive stick. We turned down my road, I felt so excited to have this over with. Once he pulled in my driveway I heard his elbow crush trash when he leaned over to me. I think he was leaning in for a kiss but I was already unbuckled and lurching toward the fresh air out of my open car door.

I climbed out of his car blaring music that assaulted the whole neighborhood, I didn't even turn to say goodbye. He shouted something when I got out but I wasn't curious enough to care what that something might be.

I unlocked my phone. Saw the three messages from him remaining unread:

Where are you?

Hurry up!

Hello…

I scrolled up to his name on my phone, pressed contact info, scrolled to the big red button marked DELETE and pressed it. My phone asked if I was sure. *Oh yeah I'm pretty sure,* I thought. The screen cleared and I put my phone back in my bag.

I crashed through the door to my house and my dad hit mute on the game he was watching.

"Hey Hun," he said getting up from the coach, "How was it, did you like the movie?"

"No we ended up seeing something else and it was horrible," I said all at once while he stood watching me. "I don't think we will be going out again," I said making a disgusted face.

"Oh," he said with a small grin hiding in the corners of his lips. Somehow I knew he was relieved.

I looked down at Brownie who was dancing around me excited that I was home. I patted his head and took a long deep breath, releasing the events of that evening. We both stood silently for a moment. I debated a way to apologize for earlier but studying his expression now, he had made peace with my cold jab at his past. He seemed lighter and if I didn't know any better, excited. I felt like I had missed something in the earlier exchange. Now he looked like Brownie circling me eager to celebrate in something. The more I tried to sort out his mood the more confusing it seemed. Without any answers for what he was up to, I steadied to bring up the events from earlier.

"So your first date was at the movies too?" I probed gauging his reaction.

"Yeah, it was," he said looking down to watch Brownie circle my legs in his usual excitement. He opened his mouth to continue then shut it and let out a long breath.

"With Mom?" I asked already knowing the answer.

He shot his glance to me "Yes, with Mom," he said slowly. "How did you know?"

"Lucky guess," I said reaching up and rubbing the necklace, I usually did this when I thought of her.

"Good guess," he said eyeing me. "I'm sorry she wasn't here for your first date to help you get ready and everything" he said hugging me. "I know first dates make everyone nervous, I remember before taking your mom out being so nervous, I read the clock wrong and got there thirty minutes early," he laughed at the memory "I ended up pulling over on her road and just sitting in my car. I think I still got there a few minutes early but I just couldn't wait to see her," he explained. I laughed with him thinking of the clock from her memory.

He waited a long moment before continuing, "She was my best friend," he said smiling at me. "I had such a fun time on our first date and I think she did too." He walked over to the couch and on the small table next to it was a DVD box.

"You want to get the taste of that bad movie out of your mouth?" he asked holding up the box, "this was the movie we saw on our first date."

When I saw the title I realized it was the movie from her memory. He popped the plastic open and handed me the box, it looked like he was holding a book open to a specific page. On the right rested the DVD in its circular holder. On the left was a small note and a ticket stub. The ticket stub had the title of the movie and theater three from her memory earlier. I moved the ticket and read the small note.

Leo,

You will always be my favorite part, second only to Twizzlers. I love you and happy one year anniversary.

Love

ROSIE

When I finished reading the note, he started explaining, "She gave that to me for our first anniversary gift a year after we saw that movie. We used to watch it every year on our anniversary. It was our tradition for many years. But I'm afraid I missed the last few." he said looking down to compose himself.

I read the date on the ticket again. "Tomorrow, we will have to watch it tomorrow," I said turning the DVD box to face him for verification that the date on the ticket was tomorrow's date.

"I think it's about time we brought the tradition back." he said with a smile growing on his face. He took the DVD box from me and closed the contents back up for tomorrow.

Chapter Nine

HEARTBREAK

"**I** told you I'm fine," I squeaked out to my dad for the third time before holding my breath, zipping by toward my room and turning my face so he couldn't see the tear building in my left eye.

"Honey, I am here for you. I know you and what's-his-name broke up."

I kept walking willing him to leave it alone. I could hear his hurried steps behind me trying to catch up before I made it to my personal home base, my bedroom. I reached for the door and he made one final leap landing within the frame, prepared to enter.

"Sweetie, I love you and you can talk to me. Even when you don't think you want to, I'm your dad," he paused exploring my face.

I continued to keep my eyes transfixed on our rounded stretched reflections on the doorknob. He waited for me to show some sign of hearing him, I waited for him to break the silence. Unfortunately for me, my dad was way better at silence than I would ever be. He would sit silently for days knowing I would be the one to cave in. He had patience enough to wait for days, but I inherited my mother's patience and could never handle the silence he would use on me.

I felt the second tear rush down the track the first one landed on my cheek. Suddenly I felt more embarrassed hearing his words echo in my mind again.

"We didn't break up," I shouted back at him. "He broke up with me." When I admitted that piece of information I felt my body slump. "And his name was Zach." I added annoyed he forgot, again. Saying his name hurt and I hated my dad for making me have to waste my breath. I hated Zach for breaking up with me without warning, I was so ill-prepared and I couldn't hide it at home. Now I was cornered avoiding my Dad's eyes, trying escape. Then I felt it before I could stop it. It rushed out of my mouth. "I wish Mom was here," I shouted into his face before gripping the doorknob, squeezing into the small opening past him and then slamming the door closed on his shocked face.

My cry was audible now and reverberating off the walls in my room. I watched the shadow in the light at the foot of my door clear away, my dad left me to cry. I never really let him know just how much I need her and miss her. Usually I see it in him enough so I don't like reminding him that she was gone from both of us. But today the statement took us both by surprise.

I sobbed in my room before opening the closet and tucking myself into the farthest corner from the door. I cried into my hands pulling my legs in closer and closer. I was trying to use my legs to comfort me, it wasn't working. I tried to breathe slowly and push him from my mind. For a second I thought it was working, until a new wave hit me and my tears rushed faster now. I could hear my dad in the kitchen so I let myself talk aloud.

"I really do wish you were here," I said to myself, the hanging clothes brushed against my neck and face. "Mom, I need you," I told the necklace hanging around my neck before I reached up and squeezing the bony silver heart that always rested on my chest. I closed my eyes tight willing something to happen. I sighed and prepared to open them.

When my eyes opened I was no longer in my small cramped closet with clothes dangling on my head. I was now sitting in a soft comfy chair that glided back and forth. I felt a small shuddering body on my chest. I felt the small form, understanding that it was a younger version of me, on my mother's chest. I put together my new surroundings and listened to my mother whispering to my younger self.

"It's okay sweetie, Shhh shhh, it's okay," she said in a faint whisper. I could barely hear the words even though the only other sound was the brushing of the blanket on the floor. I felt the shudder subside realizing that I must have been crying and was just now calming down.

"I'm here my love, I'm here," she said softer still continuing to rock the chair and patting my back. I nestled in closer until my face was pressed into her neck. I could feel my small warm breaths become more and more even with every soft smooth rock of the chair.

"We love you baby, you're okay. Shhh. Shhh." She continued turning her head to kiss the top of my messy hair. She kept her face angled toward me and continued to speak in a light whisper.

"Shhh. My darling sweet girl. Shhh. It's okay. I'm right here. I will always be right here. Shhh. Shhh. It's okay. It's okay my sweet little girl." She continued with the same rhythm and would squeeze in a kiss to my small sleepy head before her next calming words.

"I love you my sweetie. It's okay. It's okay," I heard her say again softer than her last words. She continued to rub and pat my back. I could see the soft night light across the room when she opened her eyes. She looked down at the faint light that reflected off my patterned pajamas.

"I love you so much," she said again kissing my head and closing her eyes. "I'm right here," she said reassuring me. I felt my small form on her chest begin to get heavy and now the breaths were even and slow. A soft snore started in her ear; she patted and hummed to me. She hummed so light that even being in her head I could not hear all the soft notes carry to her own ears. I tried to place to the melody of the song she was humming but it was a little too unfamiliar to recognize. My memories from this were too long ago, they were so jagged with huge holes. The more time that passed through the tattered memories, the more beat up they became. None of the shreds that were left could fill in what this song was, but I felt a warm wave take over me listening to the soft melody.

I swayed with her in this memory and listened intently to her loving words and soft song.

She continued to sway and hum for several minutes. Her patting on the small of my back faded and she started to slow her rocking. Over the course of the next minute or so she stopped rocking, humming, and patting my back. She listened to my heavy breaths before creeping her body forward and engaging her legs to stand up. I felt her body straighten and her joints protested against the sudden exertion. She shuffled the few steps from the gliding chair to the edge of my crib. When she was lined up with the crib she tilted backward to lift my legs in, before leaning forward slowly. After my body shifted slightly with the new position, I clung on to her now aware of her actions. It was as though I was faking the whole time and waiting for this moment. She slowed her descent and hovered there. "It's okay, shhh shhh," she whispered.

With her words I felt my clinging arms release, she continued to lower her upper body and me into the crib. She slipped her hands out from under me and tiptoed from the room.

She tiptoed into her room glancing to the clock, it read 3:03. She crossed the room and lowered herself into the bed careful to limit the noises from the springs. I felt a disturbance on the other side of the bed once her weight had shifted onto the soft mattress.

"Honey, I told you it was my night you should have let me go in. You have that meeting tomorrow," my dad said with sleep in his voice, before adjusting the blanket so she could join him.

She gave up on her attempts to disturb only one bedspring at a time and adjusted herself into the bed to lay down beside him. "It's fine, I could just tell it was a nightmare. Sometimes she just needs her mom," she whispered back adjusting her blankets.

Feeling the warm blanket fade I was back in my body tight and wrapped into a ball. I returned to myself still in my closet. I sat there with my tears now dry on my face remembering her calm words and smiled. "Thank you," I whispered to the necklace sniffing hard to clear the tears that had gathered trying to drip from my nose. I wiped at my cheeks drying them before a smile crept onto my face. I swam in her words and the soft melody repeated in my head. Feeling almost silly now in my closet, I stood up and walked out. Brushing myself off, removing the mood that no longer had a hold on me, my attention was pulled to the floor. I saw a small white box that had a post-it stuck to the top.

I bent to pick up the small object. It was my father's old mp3 player that was already in the middle of playing some song even though there were no headphones connected to the device. I read my father's sloppy writing on the post it:

This is what she used to listen to when she needed a cheer up. It might not be her but it is a piece of her.

I dashed across the room and ripped my headphones from my bag. Plugging them in I saw that the song was about two-thirds through. I could hear it playing from the tiny speakers as I raised the headphones to my ears. I heard the soft twinkling melody and I recognized her humming immediately. I heard the song she hummed to me in her memory.

The song pushed open a long closed door in my mind. Hearing the tune revealed a rush a memories I didn't even know I had lost. The more the song played the more buried memories crawled out. I heard the song she used to play in her room on bad days with her health. The song that she hummed me to sleep. She would let it slip out of her while she lay in pain in her bed. So many moments flooded with the melody poured back into my mind. The song was always there, waiting for me to remember.

I let the song finish and looked down on the screen.

Song 1 of 1. *This was the only song in the playlist,* I thought.

It started up again and I laid down before spreading out on my bed. I lay staring at my ceiling with a smile on my face and listened to the one song playlist my father had all this time on his mp3 player.

It rounded into the third play, I started to hum along and relished in the memories that found their way to the surface again.

I thought of her words. It's okay. I will always be right here. Feeling her words in each note. She was in this song and this song had been waiting for me to hear it once again.

Chapter Ten

Prom

I could feel my toe in my shoe tapping with every drum beat in the song. I continued scanning my group of friends and my date. Everyone had the same look of hope and fear on their face. When I caught eyes with Amy my friend from biology, I shifted my eyes to the dance floor then back to her and waited for her response. She shook her head then looked down at her hands in her lap. I felt my body diminish in my seat at her denial.

We had all been like this for almost an hour now. When we first got to the prom we were all excited. In the weeks leading up to it we had all talked about the music and dancing. We still went even though the class above us had ruined all the fun and they had made several rule changes to ensure no drugs or alcohol made it to the premises. A lot of kids opted out of the prom because of all the rules, but some of my friends and I kept strong wanting the prom to be part of our experience of high school no matter how many rules they added. We wanted to dance and laugh and have fun even if half the school didn't show up.

Well, it turned out half the school wasn't there and none of the kids brave enough to dance were included in the half that did. The dance floor was a barren wasteland due to the depleted number of guests and the oversized event space that made the marble floor in the middle look more like an airplane hangar.

As the song changed, I heard the first few notes of the top-charting song. My heart jumped up and started to dance in rhythm with the music. My toes now started tapping inside my strappy tight heels. I looked expectantly to my friends and their dates. Eyes dropped to laps where phones would be if they were not outlawed from this event. The class before us had broken so many rules and created a nightmare for teachers and administration in our school, so now our prom was like one from thirty years ago. No phones. No sneaky bags or bottles. No nothing. They were just shy of putting us through an airport x-ray machine on entry. Every corner of the room had a chaperone and they patrolled the restrooms. They were fully present and overwhelming the prom. In fact, if my small group went outside for fresh air, this space would be outnumbered with chaperones to students.

I saw a bustle in the corner of my eye, a pair of teachers danced around for a moment before laughing it off and returning to their conversation. I sighed and looked back to the large empty rectangle taking up the majority of the room. The dance floor that continued to go unused.

My heart ached for the dance floor, I loved this song and every slumber party and after school event we would hear this song come on and scream with excitement before dancing around and screaming the lyrics to each other.

I could almost make out the words escaping without sound from Amy's mouth. I continued to hope someone would make the first move. The DJ tried to amp up this dull audience again. He commented on the empty dance floor and joked that we must all be studying for our midterms or something. I sighed again feeling my toe-tapping creep up to my entire foot. I started to alternate tapping the balls of my feet and my skinny tall heel.

I thought of all the time I spent dancing around my room in these heels to make sure I could tonight without breaking something. I turned to my date and he just raised his eyes and half-heartedly smiled at me before changing direction to stare at the lights dancing across the far wall.

I heard my friends to his left talking about a quiz coming up next week in their math class. Then I heard Megan and her date talking about her mother's attempt to get their photos before they headed out that night. I got so annoyed with how boring this group was, I had a few friends that opted out of tonight due to the lack of 'fun' involved. But I didn't think it would be this bad. Half the table hadn't spoken since they sat down and the other half were wasting their words on class and something not even funny that happened thirty minutes ago.

I searched the table again for any uptick in mood. My date was making no attempt to talk to me, which I knew was inevitable. I just didn't want to go stag but I knew Scotty wouldn't be chatty or anything. We were just strangers that always seemed to have the same classes so out of convenience we talked to each other. A few weeks before prom, I asked him. I knew he was going and I didn't want to go alone so I suggested it.

He stammered an answer and said he was going to do the same thing but was afraid I would take it the wrong way since we were just friends. I knew he would never have really had the guts to do it, but I believed that he had the wish to. We ended up shaking on it and instead of the typical corsage that boys give on this night, he rubber-banded a bag of skittles to my wrist and said "I figured it would match whatever you had, you know, rainbow and all." We both laughed took some photos and then piled in the car for prom. No hidden feelings, no nothing. We were the closer to siblings than prom dates. But either way, he tended to be more on the shy side and I made most of our conversation in class. So he was my date for photos and a discounted price on the tickets. I turned to him, "Crazy how still no one is dancing, this is the best song right?" I asked hoping to spark a conversation or a dancing partner. I knew the latter was much less likely.

"Yeah," he replied before slamming his lips shut in finality to having nothing additional to add to my comment or question.

I stood up annoyed and announced I was going to the bathroom to no one in particular before stomping to the restroom at the back of the half unused ballroom.

I slammed my hands into the door and let the back handle crash into the metal plate on the wall. I could feel my annoyance building. I just wanted to have fun tonight, I knew it wasn't what we all had in mind with all the rules, but I didn't want *this* to be my prom. I wanted a better memory of tonight. I wanted that majestic night in movies with the music montage, the dancing and laughing before the whole thing ended in a blur. I looked at my watch, it was three minutes since the last time I stole a glance at it. We still had two and a half hours of this slow torture.

I crossed the bathroom and stomped in my strappy heels to the far wall before turning into the last stall. I kicked the black toilet lid down and turned to sit on the disgusting seat, too annoyed to debate just how gross this was.

I put my elbows on my knees then my head in my hands. Weighing if I should try to hide in there until the prom ended or sit with the will to dance but not the nerve. I then recalled how they instructed us that if anyone was in the bathroom more than a reasonable period they would send the gender respective chaperone in to check on the student. I crossed my hiding spot off as a viable option thinking of the chaperone that I saw watching me walk into the bathroom.

I sighed again ready to pull my weight forward and welcome my doom of a boring prom with two and a half hours left.

The familiar light flashed before my eyes. Instead of my weight shifting forward, I felt myself falling backward. I was on a loud crowded floor, feeling my body, or my mom's body, move with the blaring rhythm of the music pumping on her. I saw one arm raise and felt the other arm dance behind her hip before they switched and she swung herself around returning back to where she started. She then dived her head at a girl across the makeshift circle of teenagers. She sang the lyrics into her friend's face and her friend sang them back at her. I felt her eyes squint and she held her hand out. They both then grasped at air appearing to pick an invisible apple. They bopped around, smiled, and laughed before the song came to a triumphant close.

"Woooo!" my mom cheered and the next song started to build before reaching her.

"I love this song too!" she announced to her friend across the circle from her.

"So do I!" three others sang in unison before swinging their arms and dancing alongside her.

They all danced and shouted the lyrics over each other on the crowded dance floor. When the song drew to a close the group was gasping for air.

"I need some water," she said putting her hand to her throat and rushing to a table diagonal from them. At that table were a handful of other teens alternating between watching the others dance and talking to their closest neighbor.

She plopped down with who I knew now was my father, "Come on, not one song?" she asked him in between huffs and sips of the ice-cold water. It took time for her to regain an even breath, her lungs were restricted by her tight corset dress. I could feel the beads of sweat mixing with the tendrils of hair hanging down from her updo from all her bouncing around on the dance floor.

My father turned his knees to her from under the table, once his shoulders were square with her he leaned in close without standing. Based on his position, it appeared his butt was glued to the seat and unable to allow him to get any closer to where she stood.

"You know I am not as brave as you. I mean look at that, you were the first one out there. I could never do that."

"Eh, I just broke the ice no one could resist that song. Half the class has been blasting it from their cars all month," she said and her breathing finally evened out.

"I just feel like everyone is watching me and judging me," he said shrinking back a little so he wouldn't give any impression that he would be joining her.

"Don't think about it," she brushed it off and reapplied a cherry flavored lip gloss using a small mirror in her bag.

"I'm not like you, I can't just ignore that," he said waving to the hordes of students that remain seated staring at all those that danced around laughing and singing on the floor.

"They are just jealous they aren't out there having that much fun with us. Look at them most of them are just staring longingly and the rest are debating calling their parents to get home early," she nodded to a scared looking boy in the corner that was covering one ear against the music while he talked on a phone.

"I just can't, I would be the only guy out there anyway. I would just be too embarrassed to move. I'm not like you," he said shifting uncomfortably in the seat.

She plopped down in the seat next to him "Think of it like the lake by my house. It is always so cold, but if you just sit and watch everyone playing in the water, sliding down that big slide, or jumping off the dock; it's boring." She cocked her jaw sideways in a look of disgust. "But if you jump in and get over that initial shock of the cold, you're fine then you get to join everyone and have fun." She stood back up and saw headlights pull up to the long window by the far side of the ballroom. "Your choice," she said waving her hand to the same boy that was on the phone and now hurrying to the car.

I could feel his eyes on her while she skipped with confidence and in rhythm with the song back to the dance floor. She joined her friends and they went back into their groove of taking turns dancing in their small circle. The circle gained new followers it widened with more brave souls jumping into the middle. Eventually, it took over the majority of the floor and people would jump in and take a turn before returning to an open spot on the outside circle.

My mom had gone in several times before she glanced at the table where my father was sitting earlier to see an empty chair. I felt her dancing lighten in intensity when she turned back to face the middle. I felt her disappointment in the hope that she would be joined by her date, my dad.

The next person returned to the outer edge with a pause before a new person could take over the center. His familiar face awkwardly danced into the middle while staring at my mom with a goofy look of expectation. I felt her clap her hands and chant him on more than she did for her friends earlier. He did several uncomfortable dance moves while the group cheered and laughed with him. He quickly retired and ran to the small opening next to my mom.

Once he was shoulder to shoulder with her he turned and joked "Eh it's not so cold over here in this water, did you just pee or something?"

She slapped his shoulder and laughed at the comment before responding "See I told you, way more fun in the water."

He pretended to splash water at her in line with an off-beat dance move. She laughed again and danced with him. They both continued to dance next to each other unaware that the circle started to break apart and return to the small groups from earlier. I could feel the elation in my mom and true joy she had for letting loose on the dance floor while laughing with my dad.

I clung on to this happy moment and felt myself returning to the overlit bathroom with the muffled music seeping through the closed door. I continued to stand up and saw the back of the stall door staring back at me.

With my new inspiration I ran from the empty bathroom, now ready to drop my fears and just enjoy.

I returned to my table and announced "I'm going in." before walking the length of the room to the center of the dance floor triumphant. I tried not to glance back to see if they were staring at me or if they were coming to join me. I kept my back to my friends hoping I wouldn't be alone for long. I started dancing not quite with the same disregard of how I did in my bedroom. I envisioned my room in an attempt to dance like no one was watching. But really I was hoping that no one snuck in a phone to get an embarrassing video of my solo performance.

I kept my eyes fixed on the DJ booth and the blank wall behind him and continued to dance to one of my favorite songs. I was so excited it was still on by the time I got out of the bathroom.

Without meaning to, I kept checking the edges of my vision for any familiar faces joining me. I was starting to run out of steam, the brave blood that was coursing through me from my mother was starting to mix with the cautious way of my father. I felt the fear weighing me down and my limbs started to slow down. Just when I was debating abandoning my effort and licking my wounds all the way to my table, I saw a frizzy cloud of hair rush by me and join to my left.

"Awesome!" She announced dancing her way in front of me. "It's Emma, right?" she asked not waiting for an answer while she continued to dance.

"Yeah. Zoe right?" I asked back recalling her name from a few years ago in a Spanish class we both were struggling through.

"Yeah, dude I have been waiting for someone to do this. This night was turning into a waste. My date got caught trying to bring alcohol in and was turned away so it has been a dry and lonely night for me," she said leaning in to me dancing between her words.

"I know right, I just couldn't sit there anymore. I just had to jump in and have some fun tonight."

I shouted these words over the music and back at her. Behind her I could see two other girls join, they dragged a much taller boy behind them. We grew to incorporate the three, and another group joined. Some holding firm onto their date and others waving to their dates on the sidelines. Before the next chorus, we had one large circle that included most of my table. You could still see the shadows of silhouettes hidden in their chairs but still there were enough of us on the dance floor now that it was finally fulfilling its purpose. I saw a few chaperones dance along the outside of the room no longer hindered by their responsibilities now that most of us were in plain sight, dancing.

"Dude you did this." Zoe announced raising her hands up for a high-five congratulating my efforts. "That's pretty rad."

"Yeah it is." I responded watching the crowd on the floor grow still larger. I reached up and touched the silver heart that always lay around my neck, so thankful that I jumped in and played in the water.

Chapter Eleven

Graduation

"Smile." I heard a familiar voice instruct and I turned to face the demand. A small camera flashed in my face before he lowered it and I saw my father's smile beaming back.

I was just searching the crowd and could sense that the photo captured a somewhat distracted, unengaged face.

"Delete that one." I shot back to him when he prepared to take another photo.

"Come on," he joked smiling at me again before putting the camera between us again. "You can't have a bad picture today. It's your graduation day."

I rolled my eyes and he took another photograph pausing to hug me.

"So proud of you Emma Bemma," he said into my hair squeezing me tighter before pulling away. He moved to the side so my grandfather could swoop in for a hug.

"Great job sweetie," he said handing me a large pink envelope which I'm sure was a graduation themed card containing a check he no doubt wrote out this morning. He kept it simple and left everything for the last minute. His gift was a reflection of the grandpa I always knew.

"Thanks Grandpa," I said taking his gift and hugging him back.

My dad turned to take photos of me holding my diploma. The diploma was nothing like the movies; it was about half the size of a normal piece of paper and was contained in a navy envelope. The paper was stiff to relay some message of importance, but other than that it could have been printed by anyone looking for a high school education. I held the flimsy product of my efforts in front of me and we rotated our photos. First one with me, then one with my dad, one with my grandpa, then one with all three after we roped in another graduate's sibling that was busy acting bored nearby.

We had exhausted every combination of photos within seconds.

I turned to search the crowd for my friends. I saw a familiar face just over my dad's shoulder. I was about to run up to start taking photos with him. I wanted to get some celebration pictures with my friends before we all separated off to college. I was prepared to shout his name and wave him over, but I watched when his family changed positions so he could take photos with just his mom.

As I saw her plant an embarrassing and long kiss on his cheek with a huge grin on her face, I felt the pang that always hit me at moments like this. Without thinking about it I reached up and felt the bottom branches of the heart necklace. I so wished for her now. I tried to hide in that moment from my dad, just like I always did. I turned my head scanning the crowd to appear that I was still searching for someone. I had turned so only my back faced him, letting tears well up on my face. I squeezed the necklace, letting the shape imprint itself in my fingertips. I usually pressed it like a hospital button, calling for my mom. It didn't really work that way, but I couldn't get myself to stop. Her memories picked the time and place. I had learned this after pressing my picky call button during a fight with my friend, after I was stressed with college applications, to help me pick a college after acceptances, and when I embarrassed myself during a presentation in biology. No memories cropped up to my rescue. Either way I remained convinced one day it would obey my wishes and provide me with a memory whenever I requested.

I could feel my dad and grandpa becoming impatient through the back of my head. I tried to roll thoughts of her off my shoulders so I could turn back to face them but it all came rushing at once. I thought of how I had to hide the many tickets the school gave us. We were all given six tickets and could purchase up to four more. I gave four of mine away knowing that they would be more of an obligation to fill than a gift. My closest relatives outside my grandpa and dad were over an hour away and always seemed to have something more important to do. The next closest were further and would usually come to our events if only to support my dad in his efforts to raise a girl on his own, but this time they wouldn't be able to. My cousin was graduating from college across the country earlier that week and they made a family vacation out of the trip to celebrate with him.

So when I was handed six tickets, I lied and told them each person was only allowed two. I thought of my dad searching the amphitheater and noting the empty rows that circled the outside, knowing full well that he had figured out my fib at that moment. I tried to hide my growing tears. Turning my face I saw another girl from my class hug her mom before she was handed a small tiffany box. She usually received loud flashy gifts from her parents. It was always known since she would show up with some new expensive bag, jewelry, and even a brand new BMW a week before she could even drive the thing.

I felt tears rush faster now, I thought about how I would never get anything like this. I would never get the hug. I didn't want the box, just the hug. I continued to watch praying that my dad wouldn't lean in to see if I wanted to take another photo. Before I could find out if he was going to tap me on the shoulder or investigate what was taking my attention, I blinked after and an abrupt flash of light entered my field of vision.

I was pulled to my room. I was sitting on the floor next to my old bookshelf. I sat watching a small head with a bow pulling the fine ringlets of hair back. I assessed the room and the small girl. It was me in my old room. Some small items had changed but the bookshelf was the same as it was today. I listened while my mother sat there behind me encouraging me with a small colorful book. Each page of the book had a large number on it that was textured different than the last. Although I knew it came from my room and knew that it was mine at one point, I had no actual memory of the small book.

"One, see the one. It's the fuzzy one. Two, follow the two. See your finger goes this way then that way. Three, it's a scratchy three, now four..." she started when the book slammed closed on her finger pressing it against the smooth shiny pattern that made the number four.

"Okay again," she said without missing a beat.

The small version of me in front of her had shut the book and started at the beginning. I could hear the soft breathing and fingers fumbling with the thick edges before reopening the book to the page with the large fuzzy one on it.

"There's the one again, see one," she said holding up one finger in front of the page.

I mimicked the movement and held my one finger up next to hers.

"That's right!" she responded excitedly "One!" then she kissed the back of my head.

She waited until I felt accomplished with my gesture and returned my hand to turn the page.

"Two!" she called out tracing the number again.

My finger followed hers around the large inset two on the page.

"Threeeeee." She drew out while she assisted me in turning to the next page. She dragged her nail on the thick fabric that was glued to the page in the shape of a large number three. She scratched and I raised one finger to scratch a few times before flipping the page again.

"Four," she started again putting her hand into the book and again it was squeezed between the pages. "Okay again," she said pulling her fingers out from between the pages while I flipped back to the fuzzy number one.

The small version of me sat for a moment holding up one finger and letting an uncertain "One," creep out.

"One yes that's right!" she said with excitement to my face before smiling and holding her finger to mine.

"Two." My little voice said turning the page like a judge hitting a gavel on a case.

"Yes, yes!" she said with her smiling spreading across to her cheeks, I could feel her elation. She pulled in closer to me, "Two is right my beautiful genius."

"Frrreeee." I let out dragging the 'E' just like my mom had earlier.

"Aw honey, yes threeee," she said back to me clapping her hands and laughing a little. She held the 'E' too and then nodded to the page.

"Fo" a little voice continued a little less confident.

"Yes, that's right, four!" she responded this time hugging me in. She hugged me and I filled into her arms. I curved around her forearm as if we belonged this way. She scooped me up and I felt the smile on her face grow larger still.

"We have to tell Daddy!" she announced.

She left my room holding me and the book. I reached out for it, making her shift my weight in her arms and put the book in the small lap that formed. When she did I immediately opened the book and the corner smacked her in the eyebrow.

"OW!" she let out, "it's okay honey, keep counting." She told me rubbing her eyebrow with her now free hand.

As we entered my parent's room, she grabbed a phone and dialed quickly.

After two rings a man answered and she put the phone on speaker before dropping it to the bed and lowering me next to it. She placed me down and I looked down at the phone. After two rings a concerned voice clicked on.

"Hello?" he implored.

"Daddy," I said to it.

"Hey honey, did you just dial me at work?" He joked into the phone.

"She might as well have, guess who just said one, two, three, and four?" she asked not expecting an answer. "This little girl is a genius, I'm telling you."

"Well I knew that," he said, shuffling papers on his end.

"No seriously, she held up her finger for one and counted. She acted like she's been doing it for months. And remember yesterday she was matching up those colors to the words. And this morning she went and got me the hungry caterpillar book when it was snack time. Almost like she wanted to remind me to get her snack."

"I think yesterday was more of a coincidence Rosie," he said laughing. "I don't think she can read the color red and know which items were red to put in the row just yet. She just happened to put them that way."

"No, she probably remembers what it looks like when we put it together, I'm telling you she's smarter than we know."

"Okay, she's a genius," he said not at all mockingly. "I have to run to a meeting but I can call you after."

"Okay," she responded, "We love you."

"I love you both too, bye Emma Bemma."

"Daddy!" my small voice called up from the book before following up with "Freeeeeee."

"See I told you, that's three."

He laughed into the receiver "I'll talk to you later," he said before making a kiss noise into the phone.

125

He hung up and my mom had a surge of excitement. "Look at you my little genius! I am so proud!" She hugged my upper body while allowing my arms space to move since I continued to turn the pages of the book and trace each number. She kissed the top of my head just above the small bow. "So proud." She repeated again, I felt a small tear gather in her left eye. She curled around me closer so she could hold me while I turned each page. I embraced the joy coursing through my mom while she watched me go through the book over and over. One last kiss and the memory started to fade. I could just hear her excited voice echo "I'm so proud of you Emma, so proud."

I was still swimming in her elation when I returned to my standing position with my back to my dad and grandpa. They stood frozen waiting on me, searching for what to do next.

A smile grew on my face with her small words 'so proud' echoing in my ear. I wiped the tears from my eyes and turned my body back to face them.

I could tell my dad was waiting for me, he knew that I was thinking of her. He doesn't know that I also got to hear her.

"One more," I said holding one finger up at him.

I turned so my side had created an empty space as if there were a person next to me, then I pulled my necklace into the empty space. I held the heart on the chain there, the other person in the photo. I smiled at my dad, holding my mother's gift and waited for the flash.

Chapter Twelve

Jack

"I'm really not sure what is going on though," I texted Tina. I looked out at Jack who had his back to me now with his head tilted toward his own glowing phone. He was standing at the other end of the hallway, stretched to the limit of how far he could get from me without leaving the apartment.

Jack and I had been dating for four years now. We had been through two apartments and acquired one dog and one fish in that time. We always had such a good relationship and I could predict him and he could predict me. But over the last few weeks, I had watched him hide his phone, turn so I couldn't see, and take a few phone calls outside.

Although I was really trying to not get paranoid, I had allowed myself to console my panicked mind with the aid of one friend. I had explained the whole thing to her over drinks the night before. She assured me that it was all in my head and Jack would never be the kind of person to cheat or leave me suddenly. She seemed convinced so I thoroughly believed her until I was back home and things had escalated.

At this point, Jack limited interaction with me all day on Saturday. He went out to get us coffee, a trip we would usually take together with the dog. But before I even started to gather my things he was kissing me goodbye and out the door, leaving me and our dog confused.

At lunch, I tried making us both something but after offering up a few suggestions he was adamant that he wasn't hungry. I started making myself some lunch and turned to just study him. My curiosity didn't seem to spike his interest. He tuned out my attention until he had a phone call and wanted to take it outside. He said it was for better cell reception. This didn't make any sense our current apartment had perfect reception everywhere. I looked out the window at his back turned to me. He stood there hunched over his phone talking too low for me to hear from the window.

The day seemed to drag on and we continued to travel around the apartment like opposing magnets not able to come close to the other since his phone call earlier. When I entered the living room he would dodge into the kitchen for water. When I tried to find him to confirm when we were leaving for dinner, he answered the question but his response was almost robotic with too much precision.

"Michael's is fifteen minutes away so we have to leave here at 5:45 and get there at 6:00 to eat quick and be to the movie on time. The theater is only four minutes from Michael's so once we are done we will head straight there. I will get the tickets and then we will go into the theater," he said coldly with an inflection of this being the millionth time he had to tell me. Then he dove into the bathroom as if the conversation was pushing some secret time limit. All of our interactions were worrying me, but at least the promise of our date night gave me some relief.

We had both decided to do dinner and movie tonight a few weeks ago, knowing that a sequel to my favorite movie was coming out the week before. We wanted to wait a little so the movie wouldn't be that packed. Typically for the movies, we would do a light dinner close to the theater so Michael's was the easiest. So it was odd to deliver the plan for later so mechanically. If I'm being honest with myself, at that point I was just looking for a reason to see him and talk to him while the day stretched on. My trick didn't work since he had hidden in the bathroom right after getting his oddly specific response out.

I was putting away our laundry and he scurried by ignoring me. I heard his feet in the hallway come to a stop. After a moment, I still did not hear them move again. I peeped out of the room to see what he was up to and watched where he stood and just looked at his phone. What was going on? I asked myself before texting Tina again.

I tucked my head back into our room so it would not look like I was spying on my own boyfriend, and waited for her to reply. Just after my screen went dark she responded.

'It's all in your head, I'm telling you.'

Her response did little to settle me. I turned to cleaning our room and let my mind wander. I thought back to all of his actions over the past few weeks and debated confronting him, or calling off our plans.

I still had not made a decision at 4:00 but I ran out of things to clean and organize in our room. I could hear him moving around in the living room and chimes from his phone continue. He took another call outside; I heard the faint rumblings of his voice. I decided to shake the feeling off at this point, and just trust my gut. Something was telling me it was all okay, my mind was the one spinning its wheels and sending waves of paranoia through my veins.

I continued to try to take my mind off the current vibe in our apartment by listening to sappy love songs while I put on makeup and did my hair. I was just finishing up when Jack came in and got himself ready in silence. I turned off my music and tried to make conversation with my boyfriend of four years to no avail. He nodded or responded with one-word remarks.

Finally, we were both ready and left the apartment.

After we got into the car he swore under his breath.

"I, uh, forgot my wallet," he said almost robotic, before rushing back in the house.

I sat in the car and watched the minutes tick by on the clock. Could he not find his wallet inside? I tried to not think about what could be taking him so long and let myself get sucked into my phone. I responded to a few texts from when I was applying makeup then deleted some junk email that had cluttered my inbox. I looked at the clock again and I started to run out of mindless activities on my phone. After five minutes he emerged and climbed back in the car.

"Find it?" I asked expecting some kind of explanation for what took that long.

He turned with a confused panicked face. "Oh yeah, found my wallet," he said. He sang his response to me, some hidden meaning behind the words, but just like everything else I couldn't figure it out.

I know my confused face didn't help matters. I stared at him waiting for something to be revealed but he sped out of the spot. "Oh wow look at the time," he started. "We will just have to eat faster." He let out an odd chuckle. Was rushing through dinner part of some routine he was trying out? I just studied his face while he laughed; he tried to hide from my glance by turning to the road and speeding to the restaurant.

Dinner, of course, was no better. It looked like an awkward first date that we were pushed into. We ate in silence and talked about the movie we were about to watch, we had nothing else to discuss. The food came out too slow to fill our awkward silences and he kept checking his phone, staring at the screen. It seemed like he was searching for any excuse not to be with me at that table. After he set the phone down for the umpteenth time in a row, I saw a smeared wet fingerprint. I looked up and saw small beads of sweat along his hair peppering his upper lip and cheeks. Was I crazy or was he sweating from his hairline to his fingertips?

"We still have plenty of time." I assured him since he checked the time twice in a row.

"Yeah I know… I thought I just saw… an email from work," he stammered.

"Oh." I responded not knowing why this would matter since we were about to go into the movies and it was a Saturday night.

We finished our food, or at least he made it look like he did. He ate three bites of pasta and just played with the rest on his dish until I finished mine.

"You sure you're okay?" I asked for the third time during the meal.

"Yeah just still not very hungry," he started before oddly throwing in "Got to save some room for that popcorn and candy," he looked like a bad actor, he rubbed his stomach and squished his lips together to form the 'mmm' noise. Moving his arms I could see sweat on his shirt coming through.

I searched his face. Could he be sick? At this point any excuse would sell me. I had no idea who this man was. He looked at his phone a long moment before standing up abruptly.

"Ready?" he asked mopping up his forehead and wiping it on his pants.

"We still have to pay." I reminded him, confused. How could he have forgotten?

"Oh yeah," he responded before plopping back in his seat and searching for the waiter. He made a checkmark in the air at the poor teenage boy who was practically across the restaurant and busy with another table. I searched his face. We still had plenty of time and it seemed so demanding of the kid who was juggling a water jug and answering questions from the other patrons.

He thrust his card into the boy's hands the second he was within reach then hurried to sign and push me out of the restaurant. My feet were both barely in his car when he put it in gear and started out of the spot.

Arriving at the movies was even strange, all his rushing made no sense when he parked on the far left of the lot. Even though there were a good twenty empty spots closer to the theater.

"Why so far?" I asked alone in the car, he had already squeezed out his door. He shut the door in the middle of my question and ignored the inquiry. His fingers were speeding around his phone while he typed before he put his phone away to hold my hand. He walked with a vice like grip on my hand, practically dragging me in. I could feel the sweat from his palm against mine even though I saw him rub them dry just before grabbing my hand.

He held the door open for me awkwardly and didn't let go of my hand while trying to usher me in. Our date was starting to look more like a hostage exchange than a night out for a young couple.

"I pre-ordered the tickets on this card," he said holding the card a few inches from my face searching the lobby behind me. I watched his eyes scan crazed and he continued to hold the card there.

"OK" I responded waiting to hear the rest and wondering why it was so important for me to see the card.

He seemed to surmise that the lobby was safe and lowered the card. "Why don't you get candy?" He pointed to the counter on the other far wall. I knew where the concessions stand was, but he felt the need to point it out and drill into my eyes. "I want my usual," he said expectantly.

I knew what he usually got at this theater, but I still looked perplexed at his behavior. *Maybe this new version of him would have a different 'usual'*, I thought. He turned not allowing me to search his face any longer. I stood a moment before starting toward the counter.

Once I was in line I pulled my phone out again.

'Seriously something is wrong, he's either breaking up with me and is too nervous to just be done with it. Or there is someone else... ' I saw the text was read but still no response. I stared at the screen, willing a reply.

Finally, my phone buzzed. It was an automated response when your phone is in do not disturb so you can drive without being distracted. I questioned the delay. I have gotten them from Tina before, but this time it was just a little later than the phone would usually take. I shrugged it off and moved forward in line. I was behind a particularly large family, I listened to two of their children argue and the other two demand varying candy from the parents. I started to lose focus on the fight in front of me and let my mind go back to thinking of Jack's odd behavior. Suddenly the room spun and a flash flew over my eyes.

I was sitting in a car, well not me, my mom. She was alternating between watching the road and looking at my dad.

"What are you doing with that thing on? You said it was a barbeque. You look like you are going to a country club." She critiqued pulling at the corner of the sports jacket my dad was sweating through. I saw sweat dripping from under his sunglasses down his cheek.

The second my mom's fingers touched the collar of the jacket he twitched and sent his body and the car to the left. He quickly corrected for the dangerous and illegal driving maneuver.

"Jeez, what is wrong with you?" My mom explored putting her arms out in panic at the sudden change of lanes. "You're lucky there was no one there."

"Sorry," he responded I could see his brow furrow. "The jacket is part of an inside joke—you wouldn't get it," he said in a broken up sentence. The words came out in pairs split up. The space between the words made the response sound more loaded then I would imagine he meant it to be.

"Then bring it, you don't have to wear it. You are getting sweatier by the second," she reasoned lifting her hand to touch his face then apparently thinking twice and lowering it to her lap.

They drove for a few more minutes before turning down a residential road, a very familiar road. This was my road growing up. I recognized the turn and the trees, although they were smaller from my last memories of our road. They continued up the road and turned down our section. My brain was a little confused, were they coming home from the party? My mom made it sound like they were on their way to a barbeque but they were obviously heading home. They approached my childhood home but there was something very different at the top of the driveway, a real estate sign announcing sold.

"Did they just sell their house?" she asked. "I thought you said they just moved here?"

My dad did not respond, he started down the driveway ignoring the question.

"Are we early? Are you sure this is the right address?" she asked. I watched through her eyes searching the driveway. Not one car was parked in the surrounding road or driveway. From what you could see through the front window, the house was empty minus a few large pieces of furniture that were lined up as if they were preparing for the army, not how a normal person would decorate their house.

"Check the address." She demanded while my dad put the car in park right in front of the garage. He climbed out of the car ignoring her demands.

The house was so familiar it was almost as if the sounds didn't match the sights from this memory.

With hesitance, she unbuckled her seatbelt and was just about to reach for the handle when the whole door swung out from her. My dad was already out and around the car opening her door.

"The party is in the back," he said appearing to share a secret with her.

"Are you sure?" she asked climbing out to join him.

I heard a loud squeak when his sweaty palm closed the door behind her. She looked down and saw the wet handprint smeared on the door.

She turned back to him. "I don't hear any party." I too listened, you could hear neighborhood children somewhere in the area, but no noises came from behind our house.

"It's just getting started. We might be a little early."

"No we aren't, we are like 15 minutes late since you had to go back for that damn jacket," she said waving to the ridiculous thing on him. He did look silly in a light button-down shirt, shorts, flip-flops, and a sport jacket.

They walked around the side of the house per my dad's instruction, and sure enough, they got to the backyard there wasn't one person. No barbeque, nothing.

"You have the wrong address," she said throwing her arms up in the air and turned back to the car.

"No I don't," He said with an insane smile on his face.

"Then the time or the day, no one is here." She replied following him to make her point. She waved her arms in the air and did a full circle. When her body faced where he stood there was no face even with hers.

She looked down to where he was in front of her now much lower and on one knee.

My mom let out a quick gasp and tears immediately rolled down her cheeks.

"I want to propose a life with you." My dad started grabbing hold of my mother's hand. "This is our house. This is our future. I want our kids to grow up here. I want you to sing here. I want us to grow old here," he said nodding his head to the house so he wouldn't have to break eye contact or let go of her hand.

She sniffled and the tears dripped down her face.

"I have known I loved you since high school," he continued laughing a little before reaching into his sport jacket pocket. "See I needed the jacket, for its pocket," he said waving the small black felt box around.

She laughed down at him holding the ring in his mismatched outfit.

"Now it *is* an inside joke." she rolled her eyes.

He nodded and they both laughed with tears in their eyes. I watched my dad's expression. Somehow I had never seen him so vulnerable.

Or so sweaty.

Suddenly I was pulled from my mother's moment, Jack.

That is why he is so sweaty, that is why he is so on edge and different. I thought of him going back in the house. *Could that have been for the ring?*

"Will you marry me?" my father asked my mother, pulling my thoughts back to her memory.

"Of course!" She responded.

He stood up so they could embrace and enjoy the moment together.

"You're next miss." I heard in my ear from a strange voice behind me. I was brought back to the lobby of the theater staring at the young girl behind the counter; an older man tapped me on the shoulder and pointed ahead.

"Oh sorry." I replied gathering my thoughts. My brain forgot what I needed to order and I just stared at the girl searching my brain for names of snacks buried deep below the thoughts of my parents, proposals and Jack.

Unable to formulate a response that made sense, I was luckily saved. To my left, a much more familiar voice chimed in and placed our usual order to the girl who took it down.

I turned to face Jack who had joined at just the nick of time. I kissed him excitedly, "Thanks, totally spaced on that." I explained waving my hand to show that the thoughts flew from my head.

I couldn't wipe the smile from my face while we waited for our snacks. I kept thinking of the expectant proposal. But then I started to think about our location, the theater. *How awkward is that? Is he going to do it at the start of the movie, at the end? In the middle so I miss a bunch of the plot and the surrounding people hate us.*

Maybe this wasn't it. Maybe my mom just wanted to show me what it should feel like to be engaged because I never will be. My paranoia ran with the thought. I could feel the smile fade when I grabbed the candy boxes and Jack collected the drink and popcorn.

I shuffled behind him feeling defeated now. It didn't seem to add up. Jack was usually romantic, dinner and movie was not really the height of romance. He had done an elaborate first anniversary dinner and planned secret getaways to surprise me in the past. So a regular date night didn't seem to fit in place of a proposal.

I followed just a bit too slow so I could gather my thoughts and control my face. We walked in silence to the theater where we were instructed number three, the last one on the left. My mind was pulled to that. This movie must have bombed last weekend to be put in the small theater on a

Saturday night. This was one of two theaters that were about a quarter of the size of the others. They were against the far end of the building and remaining from before the full remodel. So the size didn't allow for the impressively large screens we were all used to now. But they were perfect for the dwindling crowds attending a movie with less demand.

We walked in silence to the assigned theater, he was a few steps ahead of me attempting to text while holding the popcorn with his mouth and the drink with his other hand. I followed, realizing that this was definitely not the night for a proposal.

I was excited to see the movie, but it must be horrible to be limited to roughly sixty people only eight days after coming out. On top of that, all the thoughts I just had of this being a proposal seemed to just be dreams, nothing about this seemed like 'the moment.'

As he pushed the door open the lights were already dimmed and the usual content was flashing across the screen, local businesses, specials at the snack bar, and fun facts on movies that were about to be released.

The theater was almost too dim to see, but I could make out a few rows of people in the very back of the theater. We approached our usual seats and settled in. Looking ahead no one was in the rows in front of us. A little odd that the small crowd had restricted themselves to a few rows in the back.

Maybe they all came together? I thought.

Now that we were sitting I wasn't hungry for the collection of snacks. I stared at the screen ahead willing the movie to start and take me from my own mind. He placed the drink between us and began to settle into his seat. He was completely unaware of the small panic attack that was happening in the seat next to him. I stared at the screen in front of me, expressionless. I was too lost in my thoughts to contemplate what my face was doing.

There was another flash and I realized my mom was taking me to another memory.

Great, she's correcting her information, he isn't proposing so she needs to show me a different piece of her past.

I blinked so the memory could take over. But I was still staring at the same screen. Where the ads and facts played earlier was now a white screen that was flickering violently. The lights came on and a pre-recorded voice announced that they were having technical difficulties. The theater lights flicked on assaulting my eyes which had just adjusted to the dim theater.

It wasn't a memory; it was another wrong turn in my night, I thought.

Jack turned to the projector and voice behind us to survey what was happening.

Once he didn't turn back or say anything, I turned to see what was going on.

As my eyes adjusted to the back of the theater there was a line of papers held up by the other people in the theater. The pages covered their faces. Each card appeared to have a letter printed on it but it was almost to light to see. I tried to focus again to make out what I was looking at. Without warning, the lights clicked off. The room was complete darkness but from the darkness I could still see where the cards were. I continued to stare blinking in the black and the letters formed.

'WILL YOU MARRY ME' was shining in glowing letters from the back rows.

"What?" I exclaimed.

A moment later the lights returned blinding me again. I turned back to Jack who was no longer in the seat next to me but kneeling on the floor beside me.

"I know I wasn't your first date, like your parents. But I want to be your last date, so I stole their first. I have wanted to propose to you 100 times. And once I had the ring in my hands I had to hold myself back from doing it 100 times a day. It was the hardest secret I have ever had to hold from you. And I am so glad I can finally just ask. Will you marry me? I could not feel more perfectly matched with any other soul in this universe. I might have stolen that line from the movie we are about to see," he said laughing up at me. He was about to continue when I blurted "Yes!" Through the tears that dripped off my lips.

"Hold on, hold on. Make sure the cheap seats heard your answer," he joked and waved his hands up to the people that had held the glow-in-the-dark cards earlier.

I followed his hand toward the faces above. I saw my dad in the first row with tears on his face; I could make out my friends and their spouses, a few co-workers I was really close with, and Tina. Who waved her phone and mouthed "I'm sorry" down to me.

"I told them you would let us know when you were done reading the letters, even in the dark," he joked "What?" Mimicking my inquiry from a moment ago. We kissed and celebrated with my family and friends.

After about fifteen minutes of tearing up and enjoying a few secret bottles of champagne a friend had snuck in, my fiancé reminded my guests and told me that we would really be watching the movie. I had almost forgotten all about it. They piled into the center all around us and we laughed about the many things he had to do in preparation for this night. I learned that Tina had to drink virgin drinks the night before just to make sure she didn't accidentally slip any secret information. No wonder she was so confident in telling me everything was fine.

Our conversations came to a close when the opening credits started on the screen.

"Sorry I took so long back in the house, I almost forgot the ring." Jack whispered to me over the light music coming from the movie. "Then I had to find somewhere to hide it without losing it," he explained rolling his eyes.

"Where did you hide it?" I asked out of curiosity.

"I tied it around my ankle then covered it up with my sock and pants," he said as if he were disclosing the master plan to a heist.

"A sports jacket pocket would have done it too," I said a little louder. I turned my face to see my dad sitting behind us. He had a small glimmer of confusion before he looked back to the screen and put his hand on my shoulder and squeezed.

I patted his hand then dropped to touch my mother's necklace.

Chapter Thirteen

Dress Shopping

"I just dropped it off, left it in your closet" my dad told me in a message he left on my phone.

"No, one was home," he took a long pause "she wanted you to have it you know," he continued taking another long breath in and out. "I love you sweetie, bye." The message ended.

I felt myself breathe in and out, mimicking his long breaths in the message. I thought back to the events that led to my dad leaving her dress at my house.

Over the previous long weekend I had taken advantage of a particularly rainy day. With my two closest friends,we went dress shopping. Now that our date was picked and we had scheduled our engagement party and photos, it seemed fitting to start the search for the perfect dress. So once our weekend plans looked like they were going to get rained out, Tina and I planned a visit to three shops in one long day. There were three shops in our area we had always known that we would visit once our time came. Tina was married a year ago and chose a dress from 'Something New' so was leaning toward that shop the most. We were going there last and had three hours allotted. I had an hour at the wedding dress chain shop close to her house and two hours at this small boutique that was more for prom dresses than wedding dresses. But either way we had six hours of dresses ahead of us. Tina was always over the top with planning and organizing so she had it down to a science with our coffee, lunchbreak, packed tissues and an old camera so we could take photos to review without risking anyone else stumbling on them.

The day started off great with, Kelly, one of my other bridesmaids keeping a few hours for the first two shops with us before she had to run to bring one of her four kids to soccer and have time to start dinner for the whole family. Kelly was married years ago and was far out of the wedding planning but they were my closest friends and both luckily had time today.

I knew this was going to be the hardest day without my mom. Every movie and show depicts that shopping experience with the mom crying hysterically while her daughter parades around in varying white and off-white dresses before she selects her favorite with a rush of triumph. I run into moments like this from time to time when people mention her or when I know I would turn to her if she was still around. But I had a secret weapon, my necklace that brought me flashbacks of her at just the right moment. By this time I was used to being in a situation that suddenly brought me back to see her and her memories. I had grown to welcome them, they gave me insight to the mom I lost so early. I knew that today she would whisk me away to see a special part of her wedding or her planning or something. So I kept reaching up and rubbing that dull edge on the bottom of the heart hanging around my neck. When I was younger I used to press the necklace, somehow that evolved to a rub. I guess it had transformed from a hospital call button to a genie's lamp. Neither worked on demand, but I wasn't ever able to help myself. Now rubbing the necklace in the bridal store I waited for the memory that refused to come.

After the first shop provided no spectacular dresses and no flashbacks I was convinced it was just because of the boring dresses. She will take me once I found my dress, I told myself.

So on we went to shop two; it was tight and almost too bright with all the prom dresses in the front and the small selection of white dresses toward the back. We ended up leaving there within the hour so we took an extra-long lunch break.

"Are you thinking about her?" Tina asked nodding to my fingers stroking the necklace again.

I instinctively lowered my hand "I just wish she were here, somehow… " I said willing a memory to grab me and drag me to her time. Still nothing.

Luckily my friends knew to pull me from my despair and change subjects. We laughed about the drama at Tina's wedding when the videographer tripped and fell when the priest was asking if anyone objected. So now that part of her wedding was clipped from the final video. We used to always joke that her kids would think someone did object and that's where the lost footage went. We laughed and discussed details of my wedding planning sitting in the booth until Kelly had to leave. It was getting later so Tina and I went to our final appointment a little early. I couldn't contain Tina any more; this was the place she was waiting on. I think it was because this brought her back to her own wedding and excitement but either way, she has been rooting for this shop since I got engaged.

Tina wouldn't stop gushing about the dresses and the selection the whole ride over. She was putting the car in park telling me about that moment she knew it was her dress.

"I just remember turning to my mom," she stopped suddenly and turned to face me with a shocked look on her face. She then grimaced "Sorry I didn't mean to... " she trailed off.

"It's fine." I lied unbuckling my seat belt. I used the moment to look down and collect myself before climbing out of the car. We both hurried toward the store to avoid the light rain until we were greeted by a long awning that allowed visitors the perfect view of the white dresses on manikins in the window.

Tina used this as the perfect place to change subjects. "They really do have a great selection here and it's huge, you wouldn't know it looking at the front of this place." She told me waving at the short length of the front windows. She smiled studying my face for any signs of her comment ruining my experience. I didn't want her to baby me the whole appointment so I kept my eyes set and smiled at the dress closest to us in the window.

"Look at the lace going down the back, just like what I am looking for." I told her hoping that this would convince her of what my eyes could not. It seemed to work, she walked to the door pointing at the train on the dress I had just mentioned.

So in we went, at least she wasn't lying about the selection. They had more dresses in the front half of this store than the other two had, combined.

It has to happen here I tried to convince myself. I knew this was a key moment and there had to be something my mom would want to share with me. I thumbed through the dresses and Tina squealed in the background about a dress that I would look good in. She ripped it from the lineup and practically tossed it at our attendant who was busy explaining how the shop was laid out. I half-listened closing my eyes willing a memory to take over.

Still nothing.

I went back to shopping and was pulled from my thoughts. I felt the soft smooth silks, raised laces, and sharp sequins on the dresses in front of me. I started selecting some of the styles I wanted and had envisioned for my day. I knew I wanted an off-white with lacing that was either strapless or with only thin straps and either an A-line or Cinderella style. I skipped entire sections where I saw long sleeves or thick lines of fabric where the shoulders would be. I got to the end of the first row and started the second almost mindlessly. I did this until I circled the first room. I turned to continue to the back but was cut from my rhythm.

"I think this is enough to start with, you don't want to get overwhelmed. Besides too many more and we will not fit in the room." The attendant chuckled pushing the full cart toward the back motioning for us to follow.

She escorted us to the back section of the large shop.

"This is where our dressing rooms are, we have one bride who just picked her dress." She waved to a slender girl who was gushing toward someone sitting in the chair in front of her.

As we walked by I saw an older woman with the same slender body and same face shape, eye color, and nose sitting with mascara around her eyes and a smile on her face.

"Mom, it's just like yours right? I mean it has the same neckline and bodice, the bottom is different but it's fate right?" the younger girl asked examining the dress again in the mirror.

"Just-like-it." The older woman squeaked out in between tears.

147

I continued to listen to the mother-daughter duo talking about the veil and the mom almost fell apart at the sight of one placed in her daughter's hair. I felt my body slow and stop before entering the dressing room area; I wanted to see them together.

"I just can't believe it; my little girl is getting married." The woman said before she grabbed another tissue and wiped her face. She held the used tissue to her chest and adored her daughter. The bride took off the first veil and reached for a longer version when she stopped suddenly.

"Ugh, could you imagine this?" she reached up higher and grabbed a red veil that lay separate from the white delicate versions. She balanced it on her head and made a disgusted face to her mom.

She laughed, "Or that one..." she said pointing to a poufy 80s style veil that balanced at the end of the top rack.

"Eww" her daughter fired back and they both laughed.

I felt cold run down my cheek, Tina came into view staring wide-eyed at me.

"Are you okay?" she asked, I realized it was a tear running down my face.

I wanted so bad to say, I need her, I need my mom. Instead I just nodded and turned back to follow our attendant.

I tried on dresses with almost no reaction to each one. Tina gushed and pointed out details trying to elicit a reaction. I just kept willing a memory, nothing came. At the end of the first rack, Tina came in and asked again. "Are you sure you're okay."

"Yeah, just too many dresses maybe." I answered softly.

"We can go if you want; it was a lot of shopping for one day." She encouraged helping me out of the dress that was only partially zipped. I took her offering, I couldn't handle this situation any longer. We thanked our attendant and walked out past the mother and daughter who were still in the main room discussing options for tiaras.

Tina always knew how to read me, so she knew to just let me get lost in my own thoughts. We both sat in silence while she drove me back to where we met that morning for coffee. She dropped me off right next to my car.

"Sorry she couldn't be there," she said remorsefully when I opened the car door. "We are all here for you if you need us." She reminded me while we hugged over her car center console.

"Thanks for today," I said debating what else to say. "I'll call you when I want to try again." I stammered before hurrying into my car. The second I shut the door, tears started pouring from my eyes mixing with the rain on my cheeks. I sat there listening to my sobs echo with the rain hitting the windshield.

I was interrupted from my whimpering by my phone ringing.

'Dad' the phone read. I instantly knew that Tina must have reached out. I think everyone was waiting to see how I would do, knowing that it would be a hard day without my mom. I was in denial that it could have been as hard as it was. I figured a memory would bring her to me and it would be like I had her there. But now that it was over and no memory had come I was alone.

I sniffed hard and held my breath so I could answer his call.

"Hi Dad," I said with pause to not allow my tears to seep into my voice.

"Hey Hun, just wanted to see how today went?" he asked bringing his voice to an unnatural octave hoping not to give away his true reason for the call.

I sniffed again into the phone.

"I thought I would be okay," I started holding my breath to offset the wave of an inhale building in my chest. "But I don't want a dress, I want her, this is something I don't think I can do without her." I tugged on the chain hanging from my neck. I was so angry it didn't give me a glimpse into her past. I needed her more than ever with wedding dress shopping. I ached to have her involved. I closed my eyes, listening to my dad form his response.

"I know sweetie." He took a deep breath. "I might have something that can help." He took another long breath and I could hear him composing himself on the other side of the line. "She made me promise to only give it to you if you wanted it."

I perked up, "What?" I felt my breath return to normal and tears that were building, disintegrated. "Yeah of course what is it?" I asked rubbing her necklace again between my thumb and pointer finger.

"Her dress," he told me.

It took a moment for me to comprehend his words. When I did tears streaked down my face in the silence. I had no idea he still had anything like that of my mom's.

"Yes, of course." I sang in a rush, feeling the rip in my chest squeezing itself shut. I blinked the tears from my eyes wildly. We worked out the logistics of me getting her dress.

That week he dropped off her dress and I carved out a chunk of my Saturday where my fiancé was out at the driving range with his friends. I walked to the closet to discover the box he had left and closed my eyes before pushing the door all the way open. I saw the box in the middle of the floor, took a deep breath and kneeled next to it. I brushed the dust that had gathered over the years. I had learned that before I was born my mom preserved her dress, she wanted to save the memory according to my dad. She had the dress professionally cleaned and packaged in this larger than life box that had been hidden in a corner of our attic ever since. He said she wouldn't want to force me to wear it but if it felt right she wanted to give it to me for my special day. I rubbed the layers of dust into small thin slivers then let them fall to the floor. I had been standing there for several minutes trying to urge myself to open the box. Halfheartedly, I was hoping one of my memory flashbacks would take over and this would be more than a dress. So far nothing happened. I kept rubbing my necklace then the box waiting for that flash to bring me to her, the genie's lamp had no wishes to grant.

As I heard the wood creak under my weight, I had been kneeling in one spot so long, I sighed and let the necklace slip from my fingers. I lifted the top of the box and let if fall to the side. The box was taller than me on my knees, so it wasn't a lid I could just swing around. The dust bounced off the lid and fell to the floor. I had to hold my breath, feeling a sneeze building up.

I stared down at the plastic wrapped off-white dress. I knew it from photos and was actually excited to have it as an option. Although I wanted more than a dress I wanted my mom to be there. I accepted the trade and turned to her latest gift to me, her dress.

I took in the details of my mother's dress. It was still in fashion this mermaid style lace dress with a sweetheart neckline and a sheer layer of lace back. There was a large train to it, I remember from the photos that were displayed at my house growing up. The dress stared back at me. I peeled it from the box and ripped at the plastic that was protecting it from time.

I pulled the dress from its hard bodice that kept its shape over these years. Squeezing into it and zipping up the back, surprisingly it fit like a glove. I knew that my mom and I always had similar body types, although I was only a little taller than she was, but I didn't know we were this close.

As I brushed my hands down the front of my dress I took a deep breath. There was one floor length mirror in the corner that I turned to face tentative at first, before turning to square my shoulders with the reflection.

Once my eyes hit the mirror I felt a flash of light, I welcomed the memory. But there was none. The light from the far window had bounced against the mirror and danced over the dress, I stood there in my mom's dress with no memory still. The image was eerily familiar with her dress and necklace in the mirror, although her hair was bigger and my facial features were more from my dad, I saw some resemblance in this reflection. I continued to brush my hands on the fabric and inspected the look on me. I had not tried this style of dress on and didn't really have mermaid style in mind. It held to my curves and I loved how it was an echo of my mother's pictures. The more I swayed around and appreciated the lace and the detailed back the more I smiled.

I could feel myself pulled to the dress and stopped searching for the memory to begin. I was broken from my adornment of the dress with a series of dings. I looked down to see three texts from Tina.

So?

Did he bring it yet?

We can come by in a bit to see if you need second and third opinions.

I responded and set the phone down, now I noticed the train. It remained bustled from my mom's wedding. I turned my body to try to undo the fastening that was located behind my knees. I fought to feel how this was affixed and I could feel myself losing balance. I walked to the wall and put one hand up for balance and continued to try to feel the clasps with the other hand. I still couldn't reach the hooks under the fabric so I had to give up. Realizing I had to take it off to undo the bustling. I bent my arms behind me again and unzipped the dress. I stepped out of the dress and saw a faint blue shape in the lining. I stopped and pulled the dress away to better see the inside lining where there was a small blue patch of fabric sewn into the bust right under the left breast shape.

Sure enough it was intentional with a small opening on the top. The fabric was a light blue silk that was sewn in by hand based on the sloppy stiches. I slipped my fingers into the opening and felt paper. When I pulled the paper from its hiding spot I found that it was two separate pages folded up. One more aged than the other.

Flash, just like that the memory I was waiting on stole me away. I was in an ornate room sitting in a chair in the same dress I just tried on. Actually my mom was in the dress, I was there to see her memory. I felt elated realizing it finally happened. She brought me back. She was reading a small folded up piece of paper, the same one I had just uncovered. The note was hand-written on a light green paper. It read:

153

Today is the day. I am getting married to my best friend and favorite person. I want to remember every minute, so while the girls are fussing in the other room, here I am. I couldn't sleep all night with all my excitement. My life starts today, we are together and I know this is a story of true love. I knew the second he said I love you it was forever. He asked me to marry him three months later and I answered before his knee even had a chance to settle on the floor. And now the day is here, I am ready for our lives to start. I have my love and he has me. That's all we ever need. I just want to remember this moment, this excitement, and our love, forever…

She finished reading the note and turned to face my grandma. She was a little older than the last memory I had with her. My mother sniffled and my grandma rushed toward her to hug her. She peeled away with her teary eyes and my grandma started to explain.

"I wrote that on my wedding day," she said putting her hand to my mother's chin, "I did it so I would remember the love I had on that day forever. I have kept it with my things since that day. I want it to be your something old." She explained re-folding the note and placing it in my mom's hand.

"Now, I think you should do the same." She continued pulling out a pen and put it on top of the paper in front of my mom. "Weddings fly by; you just wait and see you will be saying good night to all your guests in an instant. Take a minute, I'll entertain the girls, and you write whatever you want to remember or think about in this moment. It could be the perfect tradition, a something old for your children and their children and so on." She nodded to my mom before backing out of the room and closing the door behind her with a wink.

"Alright who opened the third bottle now?" I heard my grandma's muffled voice from the other side of the room. The sound of giggling women was the only response.

My mom turned to face the paper again and just like that, I was pulled to where I was standing in my closet. I held the papers in my hand, opening the more aged light green note I saw the familiar words from my grandma and felt and inadvertent gulp. I refolded the note and set it on the dress that lay draped on my chair before unfolding the aged creases in the note from my mother.

To my baby,

Today started liked every other day, the sun peaked over the horizon, flowers turned into the fresh light and the animals awoke. But for me it started a little different, first of all it started last night at 3:30 a.m. That is when I woke up. I have waited almost ten years for today so I could only sleep a little over three hours into it. After being awake for several hours, grandma came in to 'wake me up' then the whole morning zoomed by. I am forty-three minutes away from seeing your dad and swearing to love him forever. But before too much more time passes, courtesy of your grandma and her always wonderful ideas, everything is going to slow down. I'm here writing to you. I want you to know that everything goes perfect on your wedding day no matter what, trust me and don't stress. Also, when you do gifts to each other hide it from the family. We are still getting teased for buying the same watch in the same brand and color. Almost as if we have his and hers watches for our wedding gifts. Lastly, wear comfortable shoes, the only one that cares what's under the dress is your future husband and he's not going to be critical of your shoes.

Imagining the small person that's half me and half the wonderful man I am about to grow old with, makes me excited all over again. Which just means more time is going to zoom by. Soon enough we will be taking out paper and pen for you to jot down your thoughts on your wedding day.

All the love I have ever and will ever feel, MOM.

I finished the note and refolded the paper with tears in my eyes. I continued to stand in my closet in my underwear. My grandmother's note on my mother's dress draped over the chair while clutching this note from my mom. My heart ached for her love in the letter, not just for her future children, by my father. I debated reaching out to him but second-guessed it, today was emotional enough with him bringing the dress to my house. I opened it up and read it again, and again. I stroked the words on the page, picturing the tradition that was started on her wedding day.

I replaced both notes into the small hidden pocket before bending to unhitch the bustle. The long train collapsed on my feet. I stepped into the dress again and pulled the zipper closed. I could hear a rustling downstairs, Jack opened the door and my friends rushed in with him. I stood there with the dress now complete with the cascading train I smiled at my reflection and listened to their footsteps.

"Now no peeking." I heard Tina threaten down the stairs before their steps drew closer to my room. I heard them enter the bedroom and turned to let myself out of our closet to meet the two of them.

"Oh my God!" Tina exclaimed. "That was hers it's so, oh my god it fits you perfect. Look at the train, I love you in strapless." She continued to ramble about the details and the lace, I stood there smiling. She took me in, admiring the dress.

"So obviously," she said waving to my body standing there. I was still reeling from my secret notes. I could feel the pocket against my skin like a small secret against my ribs. "I mean you have to." She continued walking around me. "This was hers, seriously, talk about styles making a comeback."

I finally piped in "It's perfect, right?" I said putting my hand against where the notes rested and drawing in a quick breath before turning to the mirror to admire my mother's dress and her memories.

Chapter Fourteen

WEDDING

"Ready over there." I half-yelled to my dad.

"Whenever you are, Emma Bemma." I heard his muffled voice call back to me.

I bent down to fluff up my dress before Tina and Brittney pulled open the French doors. My dad stood on the other side and the cameraman was over my left shoulder to capture his face upon seeing his daughter on her wedding day. I met eyes with my dad then he took in my dress and his eyes welled up.

"It's mom's dress remember?" I implored when his face contorted in pain. I thought the sudden memory of her appearance might have upset him. I anticipated an overly emotional father who was so excited and happy he couldn't contain himself. But when these doors opened, I saw a closed off upset man stare back at me. I waited for his response; he didn't seem ready to put it into words yet.

I lifted the fabric and turned expecting this to elicit a response.

Tina and Brittney broke the silence, they both gushed over the dress again.

"I love this dress on you!" announced Brittney.

"I still can't believe how perfect it fit, you only had to hem it that little bit right?" asked Tina knowing the answer. We talked about this not ten minutes ago when I was putting the dress on.

Finally, my father swallowed hard. "You look gorgeous, sweetie. Your mom would love that you have her dress on," he said it as if it were a scripted response. Almost through pained eyes.

I continued to study my father while we posed for photos, each more painful to him than the last. My girls fawned over me and the photographers started to explain the next steps in the day, he only seemed to be in more pain.

We returned to the suite and snacked while sipping champagne; the photographers went out with the groomsmen and Jack. We broke into small groups in the suite and I left my friends to sit with my father.

"Were you hungry or something?" I asked waving to the snacks we were enjoying.

"No, I'm fine honey." His response was more pained than earlier.

"Are you sure you're okay, is it her dress?" I asked expecting tears on his face. There were some occasions that my mother was right on the edge of his mind, so a mere mention of her would pull tears from my dad. I prepared to console him. I was used to it at this point. I was the stronger of the two of us when it came to thinking of her. I had less time to compare her being in my life to the time she was missing from it.

"No, it looks great on you honey. I'm glad you chose to go with it," he said honestly. No tears, no pain in the comment.

What was it then? I thought turning back to my bridesmaids who were now taking their own photos in the large mirror across the room.

I felt defeated in my attempt to bring my dad into the moment and celebrate my day with me. So I joined them. We continued to snack and gush about the rest of the night. I explained how the toasts would work, I had not chosen a specific maid-of-honor but I couldn't have all five of them do a full speech. They had agreed and were going to have a little blurb from each of them. I wanted to make sure they knew what order to go in and where they would have to stand based on the DJ's instructions.

I allowed myself to get sucked up in the girls and steal glances to my father who remained in the farthest corner in the chair where I left him. Sometimes he would be staring without seeing us. Other times he would look like he was about to unhinge and just cry to himself.

I knew he was thinking of my mother, the dress must have brought back too many memories. I entertained this thought when I was first deciding to wear her dress. I knew my dad could only take so much of her memories before he would fall apart. But the notes hidden in the secret breast pocket from my mother and grandma, they tied me to this dress in a way nothing else could. I had added my note to my children on their day this morning before stepping into the dress. I squeezed the spot on my ribs where the three notes were tucked away.

The photographers knocked on our door before stealing away the bridesmaids to line up. My father and I were going to be a few more minutes; they had to have everyone organize themselves out of sight.

We were sitting in silence together awaiting our call. I could still hear the girls giggling with the groomsmen that were outside with them. I heard Jack's voice and my heart fluttered. I listened while they all celebrated and I could feel the excitement pouring from under the door. I looked to my father who was staring at the floor in front of himself now.

I started to get annoyed, the sound of all the happy people outside while I sat next to my dad who looked more like he was in mourning, not celebrating. My eyebrows furrowed and I started to form my words. I wanted to say something to him, have fun it's my day stop just wallowing in her memory. I was debating how harsh I wanted to be, the silence between us grew larger still.

Suddenly a flash crossed in front of me and I was pulled to a standing position.

I was now in a lobby, the same excitement was filling the room around me. I looked forward and saw three girls in the same pale pink dress. Then I looked down and saw a very young familiar face looking back at me.

"Don't pull it anymore sweetie." My mom instructed me. I stood at her feet wearing a short veil and poufy white dress. I studied the ensemble and it came rushing back, my cousin's wedding. We had to travel three hours and my mom was just starting to get sick at that point so the whole trip was very stressful. I remember my dad pulling over to fight with her about going home. I sat in the back, sad about the dress that hung in the empty seat next to me, I was thrilled to wear. Through my excitement, I remained fearful of the threat of returning home because of my mom. I remember being so elated to be the flower girl for their wedding. My mom had me practice for weeks at home with ripped up pieces of toilet paper. My dad would usually interrupt and try to get her to rest more.

I was pulled back from these faded memories by the current one playing out of my younger self fighting with the veil.

"I'm not," I told her "It keeps getting caught on my shoulder," I said waving my arm around showing how the veil and the dress would catch.

"Okay let me see," She said before removing the veil and placing it higher on my head so it would clear my shoulders.

"Whoops!" I called out spotting a small pile petals that had fallen when I waved my arm around earlier.

She stood up and backed up next to my father, they watched me collect the light pink petals from the floor. She folded her arms over her chest and smiled. They both watched when I bent further to pick up the last petal making the veil she had placed so high on my head flip over and drape in front of my face. I tried to flip the fabric back, but my mom realized I wasn't able to push the fabric all the way with my shorter arms.

My mom elbowed my dad, a sign to fix it, before grabbing at her temples. I could feel her already weakening body even though this wedding was long before she was bed-ridden.

My dad bent down and lifted the veil back over before kissing my forehead. He whispered something to me and stood back up.

"Oh." My mom let escape her lips. She put her hand to her chest and I could feel the silver heart under her fingers. He met eyes with her.

"You okay?" He asked searching her face.

I could feel tears gathering in her lashes. "It's just like her wedding day. Can't you just see it? She will be the most gorgeous bride," she said.

A look of horror crossed his face. "What are you talking about? Are you kidding?" he said annoyed. "She's just a little girl." He stood between my mother and I, protecting me from being married away right that second.

"Honey, I just mean look at her in that white dress. It's just like her day."

"It's not funny Rosie, stop!" He demanded.

"It's okay," She said hugging him. "I will be there for her day. I'm strong." She explained grimacing her face tightly to project strength.

"It's not that, I know you will be there," he said rubbing her arm. He paused before continuing "She's just our little girl. I'm not ready for her to leave us, run off and get married."

My mother hugged him and they both turned to watch me spin in my poufy white dress.

"She will always be our little girl." She told him. They both continued to watch me jump around and tell one of the bridesmaids how I had practiced and I was ready to gently drop each petal.

I came back to a sitting position, I was returned to the suite next to my father. He remained silent next to me unaware that I just visited our past together.

I turned to see his face staring ahead.

"You aren't losing me, dad, you know that right?" I asked now that I knew the reason for his mournful face. It had finally made sense.

"Huh?" he asked turning back to face me now.

"I'm not going anywhere, I'm still here. I'll just be married. Nothing else needs to change."

His face contorted, tears formed and crossed his lash-line onto his cheeks. "I know that honey, it's just that," he breathed out hard trying to push away emotions that threatened to overwhelm him. His eyes opened wide in a second attempt to dry the tears that kept coming. "You were just my little girl. It was just yesterday you were playing with dolls and asking me to push you on the swing." He gave up on trying to calm his tears and settled to wipe them away with his palms. I felt my own tears building and listened to him. "I don't think I would ever be ready for this day Emma Bemma, you will always be just a little girl to me," he said hugging me.

"I will always be your little girl," I said thinking *and mom's too.*

"Your mom used to say that to me. Whenever I would worry about something big happening or you growing up."

"I know," I said without thinking.

A moment of confusion crossed his face before glancing at the silver heart glinting around my neck.

"Did you have one today?" he asked, meaning one of the flashbacks to my mother. Over the years of her memories, I had eventually told him my secret. At first he was confused and shocked but he did believe me. Some of the things I learned from the trips to their past were so exact he had to know it was real.

"Yeah." I responded rubbing the same bottom edge of the heart. "It was that time I was a flower girl." I told him smiling to show that it made me happy.

"I remember that," he said wiping the last tear before it could dry to his cheek. "She was right, you make the most gorgeous bride," he continued with a proud smile crossing his face, his eyes lit up. The face I expected when I first saw my dad today just flashed before me. There it was.

Chapter Fifteen

We're Pregnant

I dug behind the communal office creamer and random assortment of condiment bottles no one was claiming anymore and grabbed the front loop of my lunch bag that was tucked in the back. I felt my stomach growl. I tried to stay quiet and prayed no one walked in while I stood hunched in the fridge door. It was only 11:43 a.m. but I had been starving since 10:30. Usually I can make it to 12:30 but today I had been listening to a slow growl coming from my stomach for over an hour.

I debated just having a snack but after searching my stash drawer and the shared cabinets in the office there was nothing that appetized me. I let my eyes scroll across the peanut butter, almond butter, oatmeal, protein bars, pretzels, some old bag of chips that has been in the cabinet since before I started here. I rounded to the next shelf that was lined with candies and surplus sugar packets for when the dish on the table got low. I just listened to the growl debating each item and feeling my body pull away in disgust at the options. My stash drawer had the usual extra breakfast bars, tea packets, drink packets and pain or allergy pills that I knew deep down expired years ago but I kept, just in case. Both my little drawer and the vast cabinets had nothing that would hold me to lunch so I settled back at my desk and watched the time tick by. I waited as long as I could but the gnawing inside came to be too distracting. I tiptoed into the kitchen and nonchalantly dug in the fridge for my lunch hoping no one would catch me and tease me about the time. I gathered my bag, one napkin and fork before I made a beeline back to my desk and sat quickly. I turned to face the larger open area away from my keyboard and mouse and set up my lunch.

I had gotten into meal preparation and was sticking to it for over a year now. Not that I was avidly dieting but just making better choices for my own health, and finances. Each Sunday I would stretch out five containers on the counter with their corresponding lids and divvy the contents of what I made into them. I would always offer some to Jack too but his schedule changed so much that meal planning turned into garbage production. So out lay the containers for my five working days lined up in one neat assembly. I never understood those jokes about missing Tupperware lids or the pile in the cabinet, since I began meal prepping these things were so tidy it was one of the most organized aspects of my life.

I lifted the lid to the lunch I had prepared and felt my whole body recoil. The smell that hit my nose was assaulting, this garlicky spicy strong odor traveled straight from my nose to my stomach. I felt my whole stomach flip three times before resting angrily in my tensed body. I rushed to reseal the lid before I even had a second to think about what just happened. During this stunt my whole body had curled up into the fetal position in my chair due to my lunch's odor. I only noticed how far I was balled up when I had to lower my feet to touch the floor again. I examined the lunch studying for signs of mold or other contamination. It looked as it always looked. I debated opening it again to see what could have happened to my lunch today, but with the thought of the smell I felt my mouth fill with saliva. A warning of what my stomach might do if it caught that smell again. I pressed the lid on tighter and threw the whole container back in my lunch bag to deal with later. I sat there and my stomach growled louder at me, I had to do something. I looked at the clock again 11:47. I stared at it willing it to be 12:00 o'clock at least. Finally it changed to 11:48, *screw it*, I thought.

I got up and collected my purse, jacket and phone from the desk and headed outside. Usually we are supposed to check with reception before heading out but I was still so self-conscious at the time and I didn't want to draw any more attention to my disgusting lunch. I snuck out the back and down the stairs into the street. I walked toward the main section of town where we usually go for lunch. I passed each restaurant and thought of my favorite items on their menus. I could feel my body lurch debating salad, soup, sandwiches. Each idea had my stomach more disturbed. Finally, I saw the bakery, correction smelled the bakery. It was not somewhere I have ever gone for lunch, but we have ordered their breakfasts for meetings and birthdays at the office. I could smell a mixture of cinnamon and yeast wafting from the bakery. Finally I just decided to break down and have breakfast for lunch. It was the only thing even remotely appetizing. I walked into the bakery and examined the bagels imagining what each one would taste like. When I do have bagels, typically for breakfast, I opt for something savory like everything or sweet like cinnamon. I could feel the memory of each flavor make my stomach flip again and again. I went to the first and most plentiful bagel in the row, plain. I could feel my body relax and realized this was the first item yet to not make me nauseous. I waited in line staring at the plain bagels willing it to be my turn to order. The line began to move, but I felt my whole body fold and a flash blinded me for a moment.

I wasn't in the bakery anymore; I was staring at a wall a few feet away while I sat there. I knew I was no longer myself. I was in another one of her memories. I felt her hand on something small, long and smooth almost like a highlighter. I felt her lips moving, "45 Mississippi 46 Mississippi 47 Mississippi." She was counting in a dull whisper so quiet I could barely hear. Finally she hit sixty and let out a long breath.

"Okay two minutes" she said to herself, I felt her eyes close tightly. She lifted one arm until the small object was in her direct line of sight. She let out another long breath and opened her eyes. It took a second to focus on the blue and white object but I felt her eyes move to the small circle in the center and stare at the faint grey plus sign. Her body leaped from the seat, ejected in one motion. She started jumping up and down.

"Leo!" she yelled fumbling for the door. "Leo!" she yelled louder. Her body carried her down the hall. I saw his shocked face peer out of the living room.

"What, what happened?" he asked studying her and the small stick in her hands.

"I'm pregnant!" She yelled collapsing into a hug with him in the doorway "We're pregnant!" she yelled louder despite being against his ear now.

She waved the little stick behind him and I felt the wet tears gather in her eyes.

He bounced and hugged her then I realized she was bouncing too. The two of them stood there hugging and hopping in the small doorframe. I heard her sniffle and chant "we're pregnant, we're pregnant!" over and over.

The celebration was put on pause by my dad when he curled inward. She hugged him tight with the stick against his back and his body flexed away pushing into her. "Didn't you pee on that?" he inquired shifting his body further.

She yanked the stick away from his back and her face. Staring at this stick, she waited a long moment before letting out a light laugh.

"Hey, you are going to have to get used to pee in places it has never been before," She said waving down the hallway at a stark white room that had boxes stacked and random piles of blankets on the floor. I recognized the room to be mine, not what it looked like when I was there but it was definitely my room. She smiled back at him drawing little circles with the pee stick. He responded by rolling his eyes at the joke.

"I knew something was off, my favorite dish at that Italian place gave me the willies and all I crave is carbs. I've had 32 bagels this week I swear," she said rubbing her lower abdomen. "Sorry dinner last night didn't work out," She said looking down at the floor over-acting embarrassment.

"No worries," he said "I'm just too happy for this to care about anything else," he said hugging her again.

"Thanks for cleaning it." She told him and I could feel her stomach turn.

She rubbed her still flat belly, "Can you wait to meet her?" she asked my dad.

"Not at all!" he answered putting his hand on hers over her lower abdomen.

"Oh that reminds me!" My mother shouted skipping away from him back down the hallway into their bedroom. She reached into her drawer and grabbed out this scratched up camera and called down to my dad.

"Come down here."

"Not this again" he said entering the room.

"Think about it, we need to document this for her baby books. She will be able to look back to the exact day we first knew about her" She exclaimed balancing the camera on the bedside table pointed at the far wall. "Now stand over there and I will get the timer on."

He walked over to the designated point and then looked up "why do you keep saying her and she?" he asked from behind her.

I felt her body pause for a second and flutter build up in her chest almost like when you make eye contact with a crush and you're body panics but your heart explodes.

"I just know." She answered turning with a shy smile back at him. She pressed the button then ran back to meet him smiling while she held the pregnancy test in one hand and her lower stomach in the other. I felt my dad wrap his hand over hers.

Just then I was carried back to the bakery. I could smell the cinnamon and yeast again.

"What would you like?" asked the young girl in the visor behind the counter.

I felt a silly smile on my face when I took in my surroundings and heard my stomach rumble and thought about how appetizing this plain bagel was.

171

"Can I just have a plain bagel with butter, toasted please?" I answered her stepping down the line to pay. I stood behind the man currently paying and whipped out my phone. I went to the calendar and started counting to the weekend of my friend's birthday. I remember that night falling in the middle of my last cycle because I had to borrow a tampon from one of the girls that joined us that night.

One, two, three... I counted forward until I reached the current date. Thirty-nine, it's been thirty-nine days. I had a happy panic rise in me. I went through the motions with the man at the register, hoping the smile plastered to my face didn't make me look too insane.

I paid for my bagel and looked out the front window. I think the man asked if I wanted a receipt before wishing me a happy rest of my day, but I'm not entirely sure. I was too focused on the front window, directly across the street was this small drug store I have only stepped in one other time to buy eye drops. I remembered the store to be rather small but I figured they had to sell them. I collected my hot bagel and reached in the bag to rip off a piece. I nearly ate the paper wrapping I was so hungry. I turned back to say thank you but the man at the register was already on to the next customer. I pretty much just yelled my gratitude into that stranger's face. Now feeling a little embarrassed realizing I was still blocking the register, I took a few strides from the counter and continued in one straight line toward the drug store with little awareness of the people and noises around me. Lucky for me the light depicted a person walking, I was in such a haze I don't think I would have noticed a no crossing symbol on the crosswalk.

I entered the small shop and looked up at the headers of each aisle until I saw it, pregnancy tests. I raced in that direction happy it was so clearly marked and I didn't have to race around the small store.

I grabbed the first brand I recognized from commercials and headed straight to the counter. The woman behind the counter had a light smile on her face when she handled the now buttery box and watched me rip off another bite of the bagel. I stuffed the oversize bite in my mouth and grabbed my credit card from my bag again. I handed her the credit card and choked down the bagel managing to clear enough room in my mouth to ask "Is there a bathroom I could use?" I picked up my card from the counter and finished chewing my large bite.

She smiled and pointed to a wooden door half tucked behind the register. She pushed it open and directly on the other side was a black door with the words 'employee bathroom only' on the outside.

"Go ahead" she said waving me behind the counter.

I walked through the wooden door and could see their CCTV in black and grey on a desk to the left and piles of additional inventory still wrapped in plastic to the right. There was a small fridge with a microwave and coffee pot on top tucked in the corner. It occurred to me that I really wasn't supposed to be back here at that moment. I turned back to her.

"Go ahead honey." She encouraged letting the wooden door close behind me.

I headed into the small stall and glanced over the instructions. Ripping the package open I could feel my heart race, I heard my phone buzz notifying another message had just come through. I couldn't even glance at the faint glow in my bag. I took off the cap and angled the small stick under myself. I successfully peed on the strip as indicated on the box and managed to get nothing on myself. I balanced the stick on the small sink in the bathroom and started counting, one Mississippi, two Mississippi, three Mississippi...

I hit two minutes and I let out the same long breath my mom had, I felt my eyes close almost involuntarily. Mimicking my mom without meaning to, I put the stick in front of my face and opened my eyes to focus on that same grey plus sign. Suddenly I could feel all the blood pulse through my body. I almost shot through the roof of the bathroom holding the stick smiling. I started a small jig in the stall staring at the plus sign and realized I needed to tell Jack. I reached down to get my phone to call him and just when I wrapped my fingers around it I heard my phone buzz again. Jack had sent me two messages while I was on my lunch turned pregnancy test run. I disregarded his inquiries and called him that second.

"Everything okay?" he answered the phone on the first ring. I must have had him worried with my non-response earlier.

I still ignored his concern "I'm pregnant, we're pregnant!" I chanted into the phone.

"WHAT?" he exclaimed "Really?" he asked at a lower tone.

"Yeah I just took a test!" I shouted again into the phone.

The two of us celebrated until I heard the woman at the front desk helping a new customer.

"Let me call you once I am in the office, I'm in the employee bathroom at this random store," I said half laughing at the odd circumstance.

"Okay, how 'bout I come there for lunch?" he asked.

"Well I already took my lunch break… " I started "But yeah get here as soon as you can!"

I could hear him gather his keys and muffled breathing while he wrestled his jacket.

"See you in fifteen," he said "I love you!"

"I love you too!" I said dancing in the mirror staring at my stomach in the reflection.

I rubbed where our little baby would be in my abdomen and with my other hand touched the bottom edge of my necklace, "I can't wait to meet you," I said smiling at our reflection again. I felt the same heart flutter my mom had, that same excited heartbeat that picked up in my chest. I paused before continuing to talk to our reflection. "I can't wait to meet you, little girl."

With that sentence, my smile grew into this stamp on my face that I knew I couldn't reign in. I calmed myself down the best I could and prepared to head back into public. Gathering my bag and half-eaten bagel, we left the bathroom and inch by inch opened the wooden door back to the shop. The only person in there at this point was the same cashier from earlier, I sighed to myself.

Upon making eye contact with me her smile returned, "Congrats" she whispered with her sweet knowing smile.

I held her eye contact and she put her fingers to her lips twisting an imaginary key, locking them. She then threw the imaginary key over her shoulder.

"Thanks." I whispered back at her rounding the counter and leaving the store.

I had my hand on my stomach the whole walk back to the office, once I was back I sat at my desk and read the time 12:01, *lunchtime*, I thought, finishing my bagel with a huge smile on my face.

ᴄ⌇Chapter Sixteen⌇ᴐ

AURORA

"That isn't how she did it in the class!" I critiqued Jack while we both stood on the side of the hospital bed.

"I'm not sure what I'm doing wrong... " he said waiting for more information.

"Well she didn't show me, she showed you so just do what she showed you." I shouted from my hunched position leaning on the bed.

I felt his knuckles dig in harder to my lower back and the unbelievable tightness returned to my stomach.

"UGH" I grunted and my whole stomach tensed. I squeezed the sheets on the bed between my fists I was convinced they were ripping between my knuckles.

"Even breaths," he started. I felt my strong erratic breathing even out, "just focus on the breathing." He continued switching hands on my lower back.

My heavy breathing returned until my contraction faded out and I could go back to critiquing him.

"It still isn't what she did in the class," I said straightening up and climbing back on the bed. It took a few maneuvers to get back to how I was sitting earlier and no sooner did I find this position then another vise-like pull on my stomach rolled in. I tensed up I heard him start again "Even—" My eyes darted into his sentence to cut him right off.

"You try to breathe evenly at hour thirty," I growled shutting my eyes and wrapping my fingers around whatever fabric I could find. I heard soft footsteps enter in the middle of my rebuttal.

"Just checking in," said the familiar sounding nurse "Remember to breathe evenly dear," she said. Then she stopped in front of my bed and rubbed my feet. She embellished an inhale and exhale to give me an example. I wanted to scream at both of them but opted to just grip the bed sheets and continue to squeeze my eyes shut with all my might. Finally, the contraction faded down before disappearing entirely. I half-listened to the nurse's kind enthusiasm before I opened my eyes. It took a second for the black to fade from my vision after having them slammed tight.

She smiled seeing my demeanor return to normal patient instead of crazed maniac.

"It's that time again, we just want to see if you are at that magic number yet," she said starting to roll up the blanket and rest one hand on my knee with the other wedged into my lower half. No warning, but then again at this point she didn't need to warn anyone in the room what was about to happen. She smiled letting the blanket roll back down my knee and peeling off her rubber glove.

"You my dear have hit ten," she said clapping my knee as if we did this together.

I felt my body tense. I had been waiting for this for months now and working on it for hours, it was our second day in this hospital. Blood coursed through my veins informing each cell to panic and every inch of me was nervous. Now all of this was too fast, I was ill-prepared. I was so panicked I don't think I reacted or even moved until she finished explaining something to Jack and walked out of the room.

I felt like everything was zooming around me and I could barely hear Jack talk to me over my heartbeat pounding in my ears.

"Finally," he said again studying my face for a reaction. "Took long enough but we finally get to meet her." He finished and I felt my face just stare at him.

The more he smiled and embraced me the more nervous I was. I needed more time. I didn't feel ready at all. I felt panicked and nauseous. I heard people talking in the hallway and knew that was the team of people coming for me. I wanted to flee, now feeling like a cornered wild animal with this panic rushing through me. I still couldn't hear Jack who continued to talk at me even though I had taken to stare at the blank wall in front of us. I let my eyes go a long moment before blinking and the room around me started to get fuzzy. I let the fuzz grow before I felt my body travel and saw that same bright flash of light.

I refocused and felt like I was in the same position, sitting at a slight angle in a bed but now my arms were cradled underneath a small, soft body. I watched through my mom's eyes while she stared at this small peaceful face that was sleeping in her arms.

"I am going to go find them," my dad told her before he headed across the room "I guess they are lost somewhere after the elevators," he continued opening the door. "You okay for me to go?" He asked while he paused with the door open.

"Perfect." She replied almost dream-like without taking her eyes from the sleeping face.

I recognized the small face from my baby photos that were littered around my house growing up. The tiny features with full cheeks and wisps of hair that were peeking from the edges of a white cap that was hugging my small head. I felt her curl her whole body around my body and her chest rose and fell while my small baby form lifted and fell in unison. I could feel that under the blanket we were skin on skin and she held my small butt in one hand and my soft smooth back and head in the other. She continued to sit there staring with a smile on her face for a while after my dad left her in the room. After some time enjoying the silence she breathed out and rubbed her thumb on my back.

"My sweetie, "she said losing focus on me with a tear that built up in one eye. " I can't believe how perfect you are. You are the most beautiful baby in here, everyone knows it." She continued and her vision returned once the tear broke the edge rushing down her cheek. "I love you so much my amazing little girl, you are worth every hour, every contraction, and every push." I could feel the soreness that radiated from her lower half. She reminded my consciousness of what she must have just gone through to be holding my little body. "I waited all my life to hold you and get to know you and now it's finally time." She stretched her neck to give a soft kiss to my forehead just below the hat without disturbing my position on her chest. "I can already tell you are going to be the most beautiful, smart, sweet girl that has ever been," she said another tear building up and following the same path down her cheek. "I want you to know that I will be there for you when you are scared, I will celebrate with you when you are happy, and I will love you forever and ever and ever." She continued and her voice cracked. "You are my Emma and I am always here for you from this moment on my sweetie." Another long stretch and kiss on the same warm spot on my forehead. She pulled away and I heard soft footsteps enter the room.

"Knock, knock," announced a small young nurse coming into the hospital room. "I'm Nurse Jackie. I just wanted to check in on mommy and baby." She continued in a softer voice now that she saw me sleeping on my mother's chest.

"We are perfect." My mother replied continuing to keep her eyes locked on my face, listening to my soft breaths.

"You two look just perfect." The nurse announced moving items away from my mother on the small table to the right. "Like a photograph." She added while she tossed bits of garbage into the trash and came back to the side of the bed.

My mother blinked and broke this dreamy stare she had with my sleeping face. "Speaking of…" she started searching the tables surrounding her. " Can you take one of us, my husband is just getting the family now and I would love one before all of the craziness." She explained in a low voice to not wake me. She met eyes with the nurse who was just finishing up notes on the board and refilling the cup of water on the table that was half pulled over my mom's right knee. She used her eyes to point across the room towards a collection of personal items stretched out on a table.

"Of course," she responded crossing the room to the large table in the corner. "On this?" she asked picking up the scratched up camera from the table. The same camera she used to take a picture of her pregnancy test.

"Yes, please." Said my mom to the nurse and she angled her face with a smile. She didn't dare move her arms or body for fear of waking me. The nurse reacted to her careened neck and came toward my mom and me to allow for a more natural pose. I could still feel the skin that was streaked with the path formed by the tears that ran down her face.

The nurse snapped a photo and smiled at us tilting her head adorningly. "Just like a photograph." She reiterated. "Just call if you need anything else," she said smiling wide and setting the camera on the small table next to the water. The image showed on the screen for a few seconds before the camera went to sleep, my mother cradling this small sleeping form in her arms with the widest smile across her face and one single streak down her cheek. The photo blinked off the screen and my mom turned back to my sleeping face. "I love you," she said simply, pressing her lips against my warm forehead, holding them for a long moment. I felt her lip shake and the tears build up in her closed eyes. I opened my eyes and returned to the room with Jack standing over me.

I came back and felt the tears in my eyes I felt my normal heart rate and no panicked rapid beat remaining. I turned to face him and tears rolled down my cheeks. I could finally hear him again.

"… Everything we practiced, I am right here you can squeeze my hand until it falls off I don't care." I could hear the panic in his voice now. I lifted my hand, an invitation to hold and when he took it I could feel the layer of sweat in his. "Are you ready?" he asked. We both heard the voices louder and the door opened. Several people piled in the room one looked familiar in a way that didn't click right away. We had been at the hospital for thirty hours and seen several nurses, doctors, and a variety of others. I studied the older woman's face when she crossed the room and stood on the side opposite

Jack. I could see something familiar in her wrinkled eyes. I stared at her while she settled in and introduced herself.

"I'm Nurse Jackie, are you ready to meet your daughter?" She asked. Once I heard the name it clicked, I recognized those eyes now, the same from my mother's memory. I gasped and felt a wave of warmth, I reminisced on the memory again. I could hear in an echo the words my mom was saying to me just moment ago;

'I want you to know that I will be there for you when you are scared, I will celebrate with you when you are happy, and I will love you forever and ever and ever.'

I felt this energizing warm feeling creep across my entire body; my mom had joined the room. I felt stronger than ever even though I hadn't eaten or slept in over thirty hours. Having seen the other side and holding that tiny newborn sleeping baby, it had given me a surge of a different sort of adrenaline. It was as if before you ran a race you felt the victory of finishing in first. It made the rest seem easy and worth every step.

With that I felt them lift my feet one at a time into the cold stirrups at the base of the bed and remind me of the pattern of pushing and breathing that they would assist us with until we met her. I did as instructed focusing on the warmth and happiness from the memory. I pushed and breathed and pushed and breathed until that one moment everyone talks about.

"Congratulations Mommy and Daddy, it's a girl," announced Nurse Jackie brushing the matted hair from my face and rubbing my bent knee.

I listened to the small baby that cried and I watched her through teary eyes. I was thankful that they reunited me with her right away, skin on skin. I felt the familiar position with Jack adding support and stroking her wisps of hair. I stretched my neck just as my mother had to kiss her soft warm forehead "I love you," I said in a whisper. I left my lips on her forehead and felt tears run down my face. "I love you my Aurora Rose."

Chapter Seventeen

First Fever

"It's there in that packet!" I said pointing my head toward the folder with the doctor's information printed across the front. I held Aurora who had been screaming in pain for the past two hours. I bounced her and continued to make the 'shush' noise into her ear. Her face was hot against my cheek and my heart was pounding from the stress of our temperature variance.

"This one?" Jack asked opening it. With a swoosh all of the papers fell to the floor.

"Damn," I let out. "Mommy is sorry honey." I apologized to Aurora. Snuggling into her in case my frustration added to her pain.

Jack started to flip through the pages that lay between us. I balanced her bottom on my knee and bent to help him shuffle through the paperwork that gathered on the floor. We both had sifted through the papers in a frenzy. Scanning wildly, I saw the familiar edge sticking out of the folder that lay on the floor. I opened it and saw the pamphlet we were searching for and felt a rush of calm.

"Found it!" I announced trying to shake the pamphlet open to read the information inside. He took the folded paper from me so I could readjust Aurora in my arms.

This was the packet we were given at the hospital with all the last minute FAQs that every new parent runs into. He searched for the section that was printed over a translucent thermometer.

"Here, 100.2," he said pointing to the section. I felt my heart sink deeper into my stomach. "What did she have?" he asked studying my face with a worried expression that matched mine.

"101.3," I said hugging her close to me. "Let's call the late service."

I grabbed my phone off the changing table and searched for the pediatrician number in the saved contacts. Once I found it I handed Aurora to Jack and plugged my ear in order to hear the voice options on the phone over her complaints. Finally, after three options were announced I heard, 'To leave a message for the on-call doctor please press nine and we will return your call.' I pulled the phone from my ear and pressed nine, I waited for the machine to prompt me to leave a message after the beep.

Finally, beep.

"Hi, I was calling because my daughter has a fever of 101.3; she's been coughing and uncomfortable since 7:00 p.m. today. I noticed it this morning but didn't think it was more than just a little cough. She's been very upset and in pain," I said all in one breath. The word pain caught me and I swallowed hard before my voice cracked in the message. "She's been up and crying for over an hour now. Please call me back so we can bring her to the hospital or do what you say, we are both very concerned. She has never been sick." I just missed catching my voice again and it broke. "Call me back as soon as possible." I advised slowing down to pronounce all ten digits of my phone number three times. I didn't want that to be the reason we didn't hear back tonight. I hung up I looked at the clock 11:43 p.m.

"Okay they should call back," I said pulling our screaming little girl from Jack before he could protest. I let silent tears fall down my face and bounce off her fleece pajamas.

"Do you want me to—" Jack started when I cut him off.

"I have her."

I felt the tears build again so I just continued to hum, shush, and promise she would be okay. I promised both of us. I couldn't hand her off. I needed her to be better and comfortable. Every cell of my body ached for her to be without pain. Luckily he could see the desperation in my face and just rubbed my back while I swayed with her. I felt her warm body squirm, she complained of her discomfort.

"I'm going to get her a milk, maybe somehow it will help," he said. I could feel him searching for something to do that would fix this whole situation. Both of us were scrambling for any shred of an idea, what could we do for her? It was overwhelming and my head was spinning with panic. I couldn't get my mind to stray from thinking of worse case scenarios.

Her cough sounded so sharp and concerning. I worried it was whooping cough and she didn't really want to eat that day so I was scared it could also be the flu. I could feel my brain dragging me down all of these frightening paths. I fought to stay present and calm her small warm body that continued to toss and turn against my chest. I looked down at my phone thinking that it had been so long since I had called and urged the doctor to call back but it only read 11:45. Only two minutes crept by in our panic. I heard Jack coming up the stairs. I took a deep breath in and tried to calm myself for his return. Before I could let the breath out, I was blinded for a moment and pulled from where I stood.

Now I was standing in a well-lit doctor's office bouncing a warm baby that lay against my chest. The baby coughed and dropped her head into my shoulder.

I was holding me, I realized.

I was my mom holding me, I must have been sick too.

I felt her body bounce, she swayed her upper body, and sang in a whisper in between kissing my warm sweaty forehead. She was staring at the door, I was listening to the soft song she was singing with the melody of row-row-row your boat.

"Any minute she'll walk in and give you all you need. Until that happens please stop crying, you're really scaring me. We love you so and hate when you're sick our poor tiny girl. So please feel better, any second, and we can laugh and play." She sang.

She started humming the song now bouncing me harder when I started to cry after a particularly long round of coughing. I could hear the panic in her voice and her desperation for the door to open.

"It's okay honey, I know you're okay," she said kissing my sweaty forehead again.

Finally there was a gentle knock, the doorknob turned and a familiar face joined the room. I recognized my old doctor. She smiled at my mom then frowned slightly reading her face.

"So a little cold, huh?" she asked crossing the room to the sink to wash her hands.

"It started yesterday, and she was upset and not eating or sleeping. We thought it could be the flu or whooping cough." She paused patting my back. I started to protest the singing and gentle voice that had stopped once she started her explanation with the doctor.

"She had a fever last night of 101 rectally and me and my husband were with her all night. She is in daycare so who knows what she could get there. One of the kids has been out a few days but I don't know what he has." The more she said the faster her words went, you could hear the worry building like a snowball that was catching speed down a hill. "He has two older brothers so they could have gotten something from their schools and given it to him and he gave it to her. I was looking up her symptoms and her lack of eating could be—."

The kind-faced doctor put her hands up as if she were conducting an orchestra, "breathe-in," she told my mom and she swooped her hands outward "breathe-out."

My mom halted her rapid talking and did as instructed. When she breathed out the doctor continued.

"It's her first cold Rose." She rubbed her hands together and pulled the stethoscope from around her neck before placing it on my small chest. "And really that is a mild fever." She continued to listen to my heart and breathe smiling at my mom's face. I could feel the reassurance calm my mom; just enough that I could feel her knees unlock and blood could finally pass back to her feet.

"I don't hear any cause for alarm. And the eating thing, that's just because she's uncomfortable. Think about it, when you are sick you generally eat less too, all you want to do is rest and recover. She still has steady weight gain so there really is no need to panic or think the worst." She finished feeling for my lymph nodes and grabbed the otoscope off the wall. She motioned for my mother to lay me on the table. My mom placed me on the table and let out another long breath.

"So you don't think it's any of those things?" my mom asked tentatively brushing my rosy cheeks, I watched the doctor shine the light around my face while making clicking noises. "We were just so worried all night. She's just so little and she was so upset." She continued with a tear blurring her vision of my face.

"It seems like a small viral cold, everyone gets them at some point, only lasts a week or so then it's back to normal. No need to go researching every symptom and worrying yourself crazy. And definitely no reason for both you and your husband to be up all night. Trade off next time," she said winking to my mom. She pulled at my ears peeking into them one by one before smiling to my mom again. "You did the right thing bringing her in, but just breathe now, she's fine." She tapped her finger on the tip of my nose and smiled before turning back to face my mom. Once assent was given my mom scooped me up and continued to bounce and pat my back while listening to the instructions from the doctor.

"Give it seven to ten days but just keep her comfy, we will give you the instructions on how much infant Tylenol she can have. You can use the steam in the shower to help break up her cough. Use the nasal aspirator to help clear her out. Call us back if anything changes or if she is not better by Monday. Again you did the right thing by calling and making sure, but stop worrying she's going to be fine." She concluded putting her hand on my mom's arm.

When her hand connected, I noticed my mom was standing there patting my back and shaking. Her knees on up to her shoulders were vibrating in a shiver, but she wasn't cold. Instead she was sweating. Odd places of her body were soaked in sweat. She was so worried, this whole time she was shaking and sweating. Now she was finally motionless and soaked.

"I know, I know. She has just never been sick." My mom explained. I heard my words echo my thoughts earlier in her explanation for her behavior. This first time was so demanding on both of us.

"That first time is the hardest. It's just because you're afraid you don't know what to do." The doctor further explained to us both.

"And she was uncomfortable, I hated that I couldn't just fix it," she said with a tear balanced in her eye before breaking past her eyelashes and running down her cheek.

"Really she will be fine. Give her the pain meds to help her rest and of course yourself too. Then just keep her hydrated and watch for any changes. Hope she's better soon," she said smiling again to my mom before walking out of the room.

Once the door shut behind her I was back in Aurora's room holding my sick girl. I felt the tears that were dried to my face. Jack opened the door with warm milk.

"Anything yet?" he asked handing me the warmed bottle.

I took a moment to comprehend what he meant.

"No, nothing yet." I answered in a much more calm tone than our last conversation. I felt my body instinctively straighten up. "I'm going to steam up the bathroom to help break up the cough. Do you remember what we did with that weird nose bulb thing when we changed around her room?" I asked him flicking on the bathroom light.

"What are you all of a sudden a doctor?" he called after me. I turned the shower on to the hottest the knob would go.

"No I just remembered something someone told me." I answered furrowing my eyebrows at my white-lie. "Also, somewhere in her travel bag is that baby Tylenol that Tina gave us in the emergency kit. Can you try to find it?" I asked while he continued to stare at me. I sat on the closed toilet lid and balanced Aurora so I could let her drink some milk while the bathroom steamed up. I tried to coerce her to drink from the bottle while Jack measured the Tylenol per the instructions. She refused the milk but welcomed the sweet grape flavored Tylenol draining the syringe. She started to drift to sleep in my arms and I leaned back against the toilet tank. I continued to pat her back and in almost no time, she had a light snore that reverberated off the walls of her small bathroom. I felt at ease now that her face was calm and quiet and no more painful cries rang through the house.

I could still hear Jack fumbling around her room looking for the nasal aspirator when my phone began to buzz. It read 12:35 with the contact registering, unknown. I knew it could only be one person at this point.

I answered the on-call doctor who asked for my information and had me reiterate the points that I had left on the message. Then I listened to him advise me to use the nasal aspirator, keep her hydrated, administer Tylenol to ease pain, and steam up the shower to help break up her cold.

191

"Thank you we will do that," I said holding my now much cooler daughter against my chest. Even though we planned to go see the doctor in the morning just to make sure there was no reason to worry, I felt much better now that she was resting and comfortable. In my head I thanked my mom for helping me ease her pain with her priceless memories.

Chapter Eighteen

HER MILESTONES

"No, not really." I answered ponding if at any time I saw our daughter 'cruise'. That would mean that she was standing and working her way around a table or object.

"Not even a few steps?" the doctor explored hoping that I would have a different response.

I looked to Jack this time and let him respond "No she just pulls herself up but no walking from there," he answered brutally honest. He didn't see where this conversation was going.

"Okay so we have some homework, don't we?" the doctor advised with a tone that hadn't been used before at any other appointment.

I felt my armpits start to sweat realizing the implications.

"We really want to see her cruising at this point, cruising will lead to steps and she was already slightly behind on pulling herself up. We just want to make sure she's hitting these milestones. So go home and when she is standing try to coerce her to come to a different spot on the stationary object by using a favorite toy or something she likes." She explained.

I could hear the word 'behind' echoing in my head, my heart broke.

"So she is behind?" I asked confirming my heartache.

"Just slightly," she replied squinting her eyes to represent that it wasn't that bad. Either way I took it like a dagger to the heart.

As we drove home I felt myself unhinge.

"I traumatized her." I insisted turning to Jack after buckling myself in. Aurora started to calm down from her shots at the end of the appointment and was babbling to the toy hanging from her car seat.

"No you didn't. That was the first of many tumbles, she's fine. Besides she didn't even hit anything she just fell over," he reminded me.

I thought back to the day she had pulled herself to standing on the small table we had with a pretend phone, small book, shapes that sang various songs, and a series of buttons that made different animal sounds. I was so excited that she pulled herself up I jumped up to grab my phone for a picture. A second after the picture was taken she fell sideways on to the series of pillows I had set up on top of her padded mat. We knew that falling was inevitable so we had lined the whole area with as much padding as possible. What we had not accounted for was the table. She teetered to the left grasping the small book page that was affixed to the table. The whole table fell with her and crashed, almost landing on her. Luckily Jack who was not busy with a phone grabbed the table before it fully collided with her small body. But the table still clattered to the floor and sang happy songs the whole way down.

The event upset her and she started to wail from the experience. We were both scared and I was overly cautious now and drilled holes in the table to attach it to the wall with one of the anti-tip furniture straps that we had left over from her bookshelf and dresser. So now the quarter of the table with the animal noises was butt up against the wall so she couldn't pull it down on herself again. A little extreme according to Jack, but it was horrible watching the small table's attempt to crush our little girl.

We continued to argue about the validity of the event traumatizing her enough to hinder her ability to cruise around the table during the drive home. We both had the day off work to bring her to the doctor so we decided we would put pillows around our couch and try to get her to cruise there. It was a longer space and she couldn't pull down the whole couch. I did ensure that the cushions took enormous strength to pull out. Conveniently Jack was busy with collecting toys to entice her so he did not see my over protective moment.

"I can't believe she said she's a little behind," I critiqued propping Aurora up against the couch. We sat on either side of her on the floor to try to get her to cruise to either her small puppy she usually drags around upstairs or this soft book she always grabs first off the shelf.

"That's just the paperwork, you saw that questionnaire she's ahead in stacking and sounds."

"But if she was behind on crawling, now behind on pulling to standing, and still behind on cruising, she's behind somewhere."

"It all works out." He rebutted, glancing down at this phone that just chimed. "I gotta call into the office quick. Just try not to stress, you know she feels that energy," he said kissing her small head before kissing my forehead. He dropped the soft book on the edge of the couch where he had sat earlier before heading to our home office.

"Okay honey, come and get doggie," I said with as much enthusiasm as I could muster waving the small stuffed animal dropping my jaw in an over the top smile.

I watched her reach for the animal before giving up and turning to trace the pattern on the couch instead of cruising.

This went on for several rounds. I could feel my stress building. We broke for lunchtime and played around before I decided it was time to try again. Although Jack protested, he had to jump on another call in the afternoon so I decided to try again against his judgment. I stood her on the same couch and shook a different small toy hoping that the novelty would win with this one.

After a few more attempts I began to plead with her. "Please honey, just a few steps. I will catch you if you stumble and the couch can't fall on you please." I felt myself become more defeated. She babbled nonsense to the couch and made no attempts to come closer to me or any of the now ten items I had offered her as a reward for cruising.

She lost interest in standing all together and fell to her butt before crawling toward my pile of rejected toys.

I shook my head and smiled at her while she cooed to her doggie that we thought would be the clincher. I explained to her "Honey you have to cruise, it's stressing me out. You and I both know I traumatized you but I need to know you are okay. I need you to cruise like the rest of them." I joked poking her round belly. Her attention jumped to the stacking rings. She crawled over to dump the colorful rings into a pile before threading each one back onto the base.

I felt defeat and tears built watching this not cruising baby play with her stacking rings. My wheels were turning, running down a dangerous path of thought. I compared her babbling, crawling, and even sleep schedule to other children in her daycare. She was more comparable to children two to three months younger. And several children were walking by now and she had only pulled herself up in the past few weeks. Again I felt sweat appear in places that don't normally sweat. I questioned everything about our parenting style. I felt the tumbling decline of feeling like a failure.

Suddenly there was the familiar flash and I was pulled from our living room to some other place and time.

"You don't know, she was judging me," my mom explained to my grandma stroking my hair and kissing the back of my head.

"I'm telling you, don't stress it. The same thing happened when you were little. The doctor was shocked you hadn't pulled up to standing or stacked blocks and I swear that night you did all of that and more. Everyone does things at their own pace." My grandma told my mom while she smiled and waved to me. I was sitting between them turning pages in a book and studying each page before going on to the next. "They don't know everything, look at her—you have nothing to worry about."

"But she doesn't say that many words. In reality we exaggerated two. She says Mmmm and Da. Not even mom or dad so it's more like zero words and they wanted at least five at this point. She asked if we talk to her enough," she said starting to tear up. "I thought we did but maybe she needs more."

"Maybe, she's just a quiet kid. She loves her books, her coloring, and her giggles. There aren't a lot of words you need to do any of that. Besides she signs, doesn't that count as a language?"

"I don't know mom," my mom grumbled putting her head in her hands. I could feel that same pang of defeat and heartbreak in her chest.

My mom put her face down and her hair draped forward and blocked me out of view. I felt a small warm hand grab her pointer finger and pull.

"Mom," my small face said to her, clear as a bell.

She pulled her hands from her face to look at my sweet smile.

"Boo," my small voice announced putting my hands over my eyes and uncovering them.

"Yes, yes. Peek-a-boo." My mom said half crying half laughing and she continued to cover and uncover her face. She rocked back and forth on her butt excitedly. "Did you hear her? She said boo!" she repeated to my grandma who was sitting watching the moment unfold.

"I think that brings you to three," she said before winking to my mom and doing peek-a-boo to the small face that now turned to watch her.

"Boo. Boo." The small version of me continued mimicking the same actions before turning back to my book.

"Awwwww," my mother breathed out, patting her chest.

My grandma edged closer on the floor before hugging my mom. "You're doing amazing sweetie, we all feel like this at some point. But you are doing a great job with this little girl. She will continue to impress you—not the doctor—YOU. You're the one that gets to celebrate her milestones, so you're the only one that can judge them." She concluded standing up and the floor creaked under her change in positions.

I watched the small baby that was me turn to look up at grandma, "Up." The little voice demanded pointing one chubby finger up to grandma.

"That's four," said grandma bending down to follow the demand and scooping me up. My mom grabbed her face and let out another squeal of happy tears.

After a moment with a wave of elation, my mom stood up to join them. "That's right, up, up," she said to my excited face once I was even with her. She covered her face again and said "Peek-a-boo." To which my baby-self replied by mimicking the action and saying "Boo," with a bright smile.

My view of myself as a baby celebrating with peekaboo faded. I was brought back to where I was sitting on the floor with my daughter flipping the stacking rings over to start again. I felt the same excitement from my mom still circulating through my body. I thought back to all our other milestones and how happy we were and how many she has done that weren't on the questionnaire at the doctor's office. I kissed her head "I love you, and you'll cruise whenever you're ready little girl".

We played on the floor with her various toys and books until dinner. After dinner Jack and I decided to stand her against the same couch and try again. Since Jack didn't know about my attempt earlier, we called it the second attempt for that day. We were sidetracked talking to each other about the upcoming weekend and what food we should pack with us for her when we went to the barbeque. We alternated between grown-up conversation and high pitched voices to grab Aurora's attention. With each switch we took turns shaking an object until she got bored and turned to face the object the other was holding.

"You seem calmer about this," he told me waving to our setup against the couch.

"I am, I just had a memory of my mom," I started unsure how to tell the rest. "It just made me feel better and less guilty; she will do it all when she is ready." I decided not to delve into the specifics.

"That's what I was saying," he said rolling his eyes and getting up to grab a new option for her to cruise to.

"I know, I know," I admitted "I just wasn't ready to hear it." I lowered my face and the toy the floor.

As the toy went out of her peripheral vision Aurora made a small noise in objection then inched one step toward me.

"Uh, did she just cruise?" Jack asked wide-eyed at our small little girl.

"She started to…" I responded staring wide-eyed back. Aurora took another small shuffle toward the animal now in my lap. "She is!" I celebrated back to him. "She definitely is!"

"Keep going," he egged squatting behind me waving for her to keep moving in our direction. We watched and she kept moving toward us one small shuffle at a time. We both cheered her on as if she were crossing the finish line at the Olympics. Finally she got within one step of my legs and I offered up the small stuffed turtle.

"Slow and steady wins the race," he announced watching her shift her weight to allow one arm to lift from the couch

"Let's call her back and tell her our daughter cruises!" he joked smiling at Aurora.

"Yay sweetie, you're a cruiser!" I said kissing her and him. We celebrated her milestone, one of many.

Chapter Nineteen

SHE COMES FIRST

"**O**uch!" I complained pulling at my foot lodged between the cup holder and the front seat; I balanced my weight trying to carry my scrunched body into the backseat.

"You okay?" Jack asked.

I huffed and puffed settling into the backseat facing forward again. "Yeah, just focus on the road." I instructed seeing his eyes in the rearview focused on mine.

I turned to look at Aurora who was protesting the tight confines of her car seat amid her already uncomfortable state.

"I think we need to turn around." I told Jack staring at her flushed face. I brushed her cheeks, they weren't warm like they were the day before but the skin was still a far more reddish hue than usual. "I know we are almost there and everyone is looking forward to seeing her but…" I trailed off realizing the end of the sentence had little to stand on.

"The doctor even said it would be fine, her fever broke two days ago, it's just some baby sniffles," he replied taking the exit the GPS was advising him. I stole a glance at the small screen. We were only three minutes away from our destination at this point.

I looked again at my small upset little girl. The pull in my chest, I wished for the power to make her feel better. I checked the clock again, her pain reliever should be in full effect, yet there she sat upset and looking to me for comfort.

"Ugh, sometimes I hate this seat," I said to myself fighting to hold her. I tried to wrap my hands around her small arm and flushed cheeks. I wanted to hold her and she was demanding that I did.

Every fiber of me ached when she reached her arms out hoping I would pick her up and soothe her.

"We are almost there. Then she can come out," he explained making what looked like the last left. The small target was depicted ahead on the digital screen of the GPS.

"You have arrived; the destination is on the right." The small robotic voice chimed in.

"Just park there." I practically threatened when Jack turned into the large lot of the country club.

The second I felt the bounce of our car arriving in park I started to unbuckle her harness that held her so far from me even when we sat together. I pulled her out of the seat and I felt her wrap her body around mine. We sat like that a long moment.

Jack loaded the stroller, bag, and my purse all together and rolled it toward my car door.

She was calmer now but still tossing on my chest fighting for a comfortable position. Jack opened our door and I turned to climb out with our daughter clinging to me like a koala. I felt the warm rocky pavement, "Oh my shoes, where are my shoes?" I asked while she protested the shift in my posture. Jack ran back around the car and searched the floor of the front seat; I could feel her urging herself to sleep. She had slept in and had a two-hour morning nap already, far more than a normal day. Since she has been in my arms she was forcing my shoulder to work as a pillow while demanding me to stop moving so she could sleep.

Jack arrived back on our side of the car and put my strappy heels in front of my feet, "Found 'em" he told me pointing down to them with his eyes. "Let me take her."

I put my hands around her small ribcage to pass her to him, but she clamped on harder and let out a soft grunt warding off whoever was threatening to move her.

"It's okay I got her, can you carry those in for me? I asked, moving from the open car door and starting toward the entrance.

We were at his cousin's wedding. They were always so close and had several mutual friends so Jack was excited to show off his little girl. We had been planning this wedding, a fun family outing, for months. Aurora was dressed in a sweet summer dress and had a matching hat we had stowed away due to her current state. Earlier that week we awoke to a stuffy, sneezy, coughing little girl who had been sleeping twice as much and playing almost not at all. I had missed two days of work and we were trying every old wives trick to get her better in time for the wedding. To no avail, there she clung uncomfortable and still stuffy. I had spoken to the doctor the day before and they had advised that we could attend the wedding but should take it easy. She was still on the mend. Her fever was gone and she was improving every day, just not in time to say she was better today. After debating back and forth we finally decided we would try to bring her and just leave if it wasn't working.

So in we went.

We arrived a little early just in case there was a last minute change or outfit mishap that we had to resolve. So upon arrival the photographer was still parading the groomsmen around the foyer and stairs leading to the ballroom. We were ushered into a waiting area with a small bar and large windows that glared into Aurora's eyes. She complained and flipped her head so she was now breathing on my neck. I could now feel the long string of drool she left on my left strap running down to my ribs.

"I'm gonna try to catch Tim." Jack told me pointing to the groom smiling at a photographer not three feet from the door we just entered. I nodded taking a seat in the small bistro chair and leaning back as far as I could without slipping off the seat.

I felt Aurora instantly become heavier; sleep was starting to take over.

I watched Jack congratulate Tim and hug him before pointing over to us in the chair. I nodded my head over to them both, vigilant not to disturb Aurora with my movement. Jack returned and he pointed up to the small stick figure man depicting the restroom. I nodded to him again careful not to move any other part of us in the chair.

I waited for him to return and listened to her breaths getting deeper and steadier. Now much more comfortable, I felt her thumb fall from her mouth and lay sopping on my collarbone. I sighed knowing she was at least comfortable and resting. Ideally she would have slept in the car but I would accept any sleep at this point.

Jack came out of the bathroom and smiled down to us. I saw him opening his mouth to tell me something. I rushed to make a 'shhh' face without the finger pointing my eyes at her sleeping on me before returning my glance to him, expecting the movement to be understood.

"Sleeping?" he whispered once he was close enough to us.

I gave a light nod and waited for her to protest the movement. She was asleep enough to let it go unnoticed.

"What should we do?" he whispered glancing at the time on his phone and looking to the small groups of family and friends that started toward the entrance.

"I think we have to let her sleep, we can try to put her in the stroller…" I whispered and I slowly stood up. When I tilted forward to lower her into the stroller, she bristled and grabbed on furious before letting out a little creak of a cry. I pulled her back into me feeling the fresh drool drying on the front of my dress now. "Or not." I continued "You go; I can stay here with her until she wakes up."

He stared at me waiting for another option to be offered.

"It's fine, I will join you after she's awake. She needs her rest more than she needs to be a witness to nuptials." I whispered to him before turning and lowering myself in the same seat at the awkward angle I was previously.

"You have your phone if you need me, I will be right over there, I think that is where the whole thing is going down," he motioned to the corner where groups of family and friends were being led.

"Yeah, it's in my bag." I pointed my chin toward the small glittery bag balanced on top of the stroller.

"You sure? I can stay with you both." He followed up staring down at us.

"It's fine; he's one of your closest friends. You can't miss his big day," I said smiling up at him.

He kissed my lips before kissing the back of her head. She let out a small snort, asserting that this was the best plan. Then he joined the most recent group being ushered down the hall.

As more groups started to arrive the foyer started to come to life. Excited voices welcoming each other while they hugged and kissed. Several family members and friends of Jack had stopped at the bar or seen me from the entrance. They alternated between waving from afar or coming close before pantomiming sleep and stepping away on their tiptoes as if they were the only sound in the room.

The noise grew to a steady stream of heels and voices, I felt Aurora push into me more willing for the disturbance to go away. I started to peer around for an option or farther corner, but nothing seemed to be an improvement. A waitress popped out of nowhere and slipped over to my table before lowering an ice water.

"So sweet," she whispered to me backing up after her delivery. "You know if it is a little too loud in here, we have a second bride's room that won't be used today since we only have the one wedding. You can sit in there with her if you want to be comfy, and have some quiet." She explained waving to the growing crowd creating the noise.

"Uh yeah, that would be great. Thank you," I said almost without thought. I could feel my butt falling asleep on the edge of the chair and Aurora was growing more impatient with the noisy surroundings.

"Of course. Luckily it's on this floor just over here." She explained pushing the stroller. I followed behind, trusting this stranger. I watched her push open the doors to a grand ballroom that was completely empty of all tables, decorations, and chairs. It was the most bizarre way to see a ballroom, so bare and naked. "Usually we have two weddings, but as fate would have it, it's just the one today so no one will be making any noise down here." She explained making a sharp left toward an intricate door with a wedding dress cutout on it. She opened the door and I saw the plush couch on the far wall along with several small tables, makeup mirrors, and a large TV.

I practically sprinted to the couch feeling my arm protest the weight of Aurora, I had locked my elbow to minimize the movement that jarred her since we arrived.

She pushed the stroller next to me before putting down the same glass of water from earlier in the small cup holder so that it was even with where I sat.

"Thank you so much." I whispered to her trying to contort my face to show the level of gratitude I had. I hope she was able to understand from my small squint and drawn out 'so'.

"No problem." She waved off, not recognizing her own heroic efforts. "Do you want anything else?" she asked.

"Oh, my phone can you just pull my phone out of the front pocket of that bag." I motioned to my bag on top of the stroller.

"Sure" she replied before sliding the phone out and putting it in my now outstretched arm. I had taken the opportunity to lean back and balance Aurora on my chest and only needed one hand to keep her in place. Once she handed me the phone she smiled again and tiptoed out of the room, she closed the door behind her. I no longer heard the clamoring outside.

I took a moment to take a quick selfie, before texting the image to Jack.

The bartender just brought me to my own private room. We are in the other Bride room through the doors next to where I was sitting.

I texted him and waited for his response.

Wow perfect. Need anything? He replied.

No, just take lots of pictures. I responded before adding the camera and ring emoji.

I sighed and looked up at the ceiling. I could vaguely hear instrumental music pick up on the far end of the building. I put my hand on Aurora's soft small back and brushed my hand up and down. Now that we were fully settled, I closed my eyes. It was such a relief to have her comfortable again, I could care less about the wedding I was missing, the champagne, the laughter that was about to pick up on the other end of the club. I just sat on the soft couch listening to her breath over the sound of the wedding progressing outside.

Suddenly I was blinded and pulled from the white decorative room. I was sitting up in a hoodie realizing I was transported to my mom again. I saw my own face through her eyes looking up.

The face was tinted green and it swayed with the waves I now felt underneath where they sat.

"It's okay sweetie, come here," she said embracing me, I accepted the hug. I was also in a hoodie, the wind whipped around us and you could hear the engine shaking through her eardrums. I realized we were on a boat and I had a glimmer of a memory from my past.

I remembered the boat ride. I remember the cold wind whipping my baby hairs around the frame of my face into my

209

eyes. I remembered the queasy feeling that took over me. I could see the discomfort on my young face. She picked me up and wrapped my long legs around her waist carrying me toward a small tower on the boat.

"Are you okay?" she asked feeling my body pull away without warning. She felt my stomach muscles tense and release, now with panic she rushed to turn my body toward a large trash bin. I threw up almost into the trash can she had aimed me at just a second too late. She ripped her hoodie off, turned the whole thing inside out and cleaned my face.

Now I really remember this boat ride. I hated it. I remember being so excited to go out and wanted to see dolphins, seals, and whales but once we were out on the water I got sick and I hated the whole thing. I didn't remember the end of it anymore but I remember the middle quite vividly. I think it was my first time having motion sickness and after that, I was always a little more susceptible.

"It's okay honey don't worry, it's all gone," she told me wiping my mouth and giving me some water to sip. "I'm just going to talk to the captain quick; you want to hold my hand?" She asked me in her most soothing voice before straightening back up and banging on a small door to the tower we had walked to. While waiting for someone inside to react to her rapping on the small window, I felt the world spin just a moment.

The man with the hat embroidered 'Captain' turned and waved, obviously posing for a photo. She wasn't there to take a photo. My mom stared at him and pointed to the door handle through the small port window that only showed her face. He held up one finger before speaking to a man standing at the controls. Then he looked back to my mom and sauntered over to open the latch. He opened it just enough so that her voice could carry in and no more.

"Good Evening captain, can we turn this damn thing around already," she said as if they were old friends before pushing in so that her right shoulder and head could enter the space.

"Excuse me, ma'am, you aren't permitted to..."

"Not sure if you were aware, but most of your boat is now green including my daughter. It's time to call this one," she said pushing the door again and edging more into the small opening.

The captain squinted his eyes at her pressing his lips together settling in to ignore her comments.

I felt a small tug on my mother's left hand; she swung back out of the door and lifted me up just in time for me to throw up into another garbage can.

When she did, I felt the pang of nausea. I felt her mouth fill with saliva threatening to join me in puking into the garbage. She swallowed hard lowering down to my level and cleaning my face and hair with her inside-out hoodie again.

"Just one more second sweetie, then we are going home, okay?" she asked without waiting for a reply. She turned back to the door only to see it back to its original position, closed.

She banged hard on the door with her free hand before turning back to smile at me. This time when she flipped her head between me and the door, I felt the spin in her head and the pull of her stomach twisting angrily. I could feel the cold air against her while she held her soiled hoodie and waited for the captain again. She fought against the cold and nausea ignoring her instincts.

The captain opened the door expecting her upper body to push in again. He gave enough space for the persistent stranger, readying himself to deal with her.

"Ma'am…" he started putting his arms in front of him, warning her this would be their last exchange.

"No, you are bringing this boat back. Half the people are just as sick as my daughter, but I don't care about them. I care about her. And I hate nothing more than seeing her unhappy or sick. So I will make you hate nothing more than me if you don't bring us back now!" She told him without blinking. I felt her head spin and she stared at him waiting for his assent.

"We can't just do that…" he started.

"The way I see it, if someone were to fall overboard, you would have to go back. Right? That water looks too cold to not bring them back after falling in." she threatened waving to the frigid water that continued to raise and lower the boat. Each wave swayed her and made her stomach lurch but she continued to stand steady, staring at the captain.

He studied her face, no doubt because it had to be green at this point with the feeling that gripped her insides.

"Don't make me get my hair wet." She continued bending down to untie her shoes. I felt her mouth again fill with warm saliva from the change in altitude. She placed her shoes neatly against the wall nearest the door and the captain stared transfixed at her threat.

When she stood up, he rolled his eyes and closed the door behind him. He crossed to the middle of the small room and grabbed a loose corded phone receiver, maintaining eye contact with my mom. She stared back at him waiting for his next move.

Ding "Ladies and gentlemen, it seems the weather is continuing to be a problem this afternoon. We are going to need to return to shore at this time. Please prepare to de-board and collect your belongings," he stated into the microphone continuing to stare at her. The second ding chimed signaling the end of his message. He nodded to my mom who had just swallowed hard.

"See honey we will be back on shore soon, okay? Let's go sit back down." She told me, I felt her breath get cut short by a small gag building in her throat. She slipped her feet back into her shoes and tied them before holding out her hand again for me.

"Okay Mommy" I replied standing there pale now that the green had faded from my face. We walked to the closest open seats and she balled up the soiled hoodie then picked me up onto her lap.

She sat there humming into my ear until we approached the same pier we had left earlier. The crew tied the boat to the dock but she waited swallowing strategically. She watched the other passengers celebrate the early return from the rocky water; most of them were obviously recovering before they shuffled off the boat. I heard a soft snore coming from myself in her arms when she picked me up and crept down the stairs. She turned the corner and we saw the captain from earlier nodding as people disembarked. They were all equally satisfied to return to the shore. The ride was bouncy and brutal and we weren't the only green faces on board. She nodded to the captain and mouthed something over my sleeping head.

"You're welcome," he said nodding back.

"No! Puke bag!" she said with volume and more urgency.

He scrambled around where he stood before finding a small white paper bag and pushing it into her outstretched arm. Balancing me with one arm, she slammed the bag to her mouth with her free hand and puked violently into it.

She nodded to the shocked captain with as much dignity that she could muster before throwing the bag into a garbage can a few steps in front of her. She then slipped the hoodie from between us and smooshed her face into the fabric before throwing the hoodie into the same trash.

She nodded again completing the show for the captain and his crew, before walking off the boat with me sleeping in her arms.

I was transported back to under my sleeping little girl. I sighed feeling her comfort and could see her peaceful face. I kissed her soft warm forehead and smiled thinking of my memory of that horrible boat ride. I never knew my mom got the whole boat turned around or that she threw up while carrying me. No wonder I didn't remember the tail end of that trip, I was asleep. I let out a little giggle thinking of my bold brash mom and what she did for me before I kissed Aurora once more and laid my head back.

I was almost positive she would have jumped in the water to get me to shore. I know I would for Aurora.

Chapter Twenty

So Proud

"She did it, did you see?" I half screamed at Jack slapping his shoulder without looking at him. I did not break eye contact from Aurora.

"I'm watching, I'm watching," he responded sitting up a little straighter with me on the floor.

We were both sitting cramped on the floor outside of the tub watching our tiny little girl count to five on her fingers for the third time.

"One, two, threeee, four, fie," she said again touching her pointer finger to each of her fingers on her left hand. She finished and clapped a few times before starting the pattern over.

Jack and I sat there squealing "Yes honey, that's it. Good job. What a smarty you are." We rang together staring at her in wonderment.

She did this little show four more times before turning to us and stating "All done" raising her arms to us to be lifted from the tub.

She was a pruned little girl at this point. We were both so caught up in the fact that she was counting that in all the excitement, we hadn't rinsed her hair. She sat there arms outstretched waiting for us to pull her from the cooling bathwater. I stood up to pluck her from the water.

"That's right sweetie, all done, one, two, three, four, five. All done." I sang holding her damp body to mine and danced around each syllable.

Jack stood up next to us while I celebrated and told Aurora she was such a little genius and we are so proud of her. I clued in to him once he cleared his throat.

"What?" I asked studying his face. He was staring at me expectantly.

"Not all done just yet," he explained pointing to her hair still filled with bubbles that had yet to be rinsed.

"Oh." I exclaimed I plopping her back into the tub. "Sorry Rorey, you had me so excited, Mommy didn't even notice." I explained to her dipping her head back and running a cup full of the chilled bathwater over her hair. I did this a few times until the water ran clear without bubbles and her hair no longer felt slimy to the touch. Then I swooped her up again and wrapped her up in her fluffy pink robe before carrying her to her room to dress her.

"Maybe I should take it from here." Jack told me pointing to my soaked shirt. In all the excitement I had pulled her from the tub, soapy, and wet and held her against me like usual without any concern for my clothes. I was now dripping and my shoulder was covered in popping bubbles.

I continued in a sing-song tone to her "Daddy is going to get you all dried off my little genius. I'm all soapy my little Rorey girl."

I danced from the room so excited to have witnessed her counting. I continued to gloat to Jack who was there for the whole thing.

"Can you believe that she did all the way to five, she skipped right past three? She is seriously a genius, it's not a parenting bias anymore, she's a genius." I called to him from our room grabbing a shirt out of my top drawer and throwing it on backward to race back to my little girl.

I bounced around next to Jack who calmly let me celebrate while he pushed her pajamas over her head.

"One, two, three, four, five," I said in front of her touching each finger.

She had one arm free and the other still trapped in the shirt but she started mimicking me again, "One, two, threeee, four, fie."

"Slow down sweetie, let Daddy get your PJs on." Jack instructed fighting to catch her moving hand to slide it through the other armhole. He let go and she started again. "One, two, threeee, four, fie."

I jumped to my feet, "What are we doing we have to get this on film." I shouted at them both before bolting from the room to grab my phone where it lay on the charger in my room. I pulled the cord from my phone and a bright light flashed in from of me before I felt that familiar pull.

I blinked and I was in my childhood playroom. The room that became my mother's when she got sick. I was looking at myself as a young girl from across the room. I stood with one hand balancing me and the other spread across my lips. I threw the hand on my lips in the air, blowing a kiss.

"Yayyy, yes Emma, muahhhh." My mother called back to me mimicking the same movement back. "Muah," she said again while she dramatically blew me a kiss.

I copied her and she continued to jump around and perform the same over the top kiss with sound effect.

I listened to her encourage me "My smart little Emma Bemma, you make me so proud! You learned that today my little genius." She sang my praises watching me do the same sloppy blown kiss.

When she clapped encouraging me this time I heard a rustle outside.

"Leo, is that you? You have to get in here." She called out so her voice would carry to the creator of the rustling noise. I heard a little more noise as things were put down on our kitchen counter, before the echoing sound of footsteps started toward the playroom. I saw a shadow appear next to my mom but she did not turn to my dad who had joined them.

"Muah," she said kissing her hand before blowing the kiss to me across the room.

I watched myself as a toddler point excitedly to my dad "Da." I exclaimed taking the few steps to meet him and falling to my hands.

She rushed to close the space to where I was on all fours and turned to my dad. "You just missed it she's been blowing kisses all afternoon. She also learned how to do the happy dance today. She's been our little all-star." She sang stealing a fast glance at him before she could look at me again. "Muah." she announced blowing him a kiss while still watching me on the floor.

I was staring up at my dad while my mother blew more kisses waving her arm through the air.

"What's the happy dance?" he asked joining our small party sitting on the floor before he kissed the top of my head then kissed my mother's.

"You know, if you're happy and you know it clap your hands." She started and she paused to clap. I heard three excited claps come from my small self who was smiling at them both.

"See, you see. Did you hear her? She did it too!" my mother shrieked at him and slapped his arm closest to her.

"Ow," he said rubbing the spot where she just hit. "I saw her, I am sitting right here you know?"

"Sorry, I know. But can you believe it? Look at this little girl could you be more proud. She is our little genius," she said adjusting her seat on the floor so she could face them both.

"If you're happy and you know it clap your hands." She continued pausing to clap. When she clapped so did I and the two of them celebrated.

"If you're happy and you know and you really want to show it. If you're happy and you know it clap your hands." She sang the rest before I clapped again on cue. I let out a little giggle knowing this was the end of the song and clapped more. My parents celebrated with their own applause. I watched the young version of me relish in their enthusiasm and beam back to them.

"You know she is this close," she said pinching her fingers together depicting a small space "from patty-cake too." She announced, "She is just our little smartie, I'm telling you." Then she turned back to face me.

219

Once she did, I watched my small bright eyes search the scene in front of me curious before I put my hand over my lips made a long drawn out 'mmm' noise then threw my hand to my parents, blowing them a kiss.

"You see! She wasn't doing the noise this morning! Did you see her?" my mother shouted to my father before slapping him on the arm again.

"Ow," he said again to her "I'm still right here, I saw it honey," he said and he turned to me and blew a kiss back. "Mwah, good job Emma Bemma."

I basked in the feeling my mother had while I watched this memory unfold. I could feel her excitement and her body danced around in its own skin. I felt her pride every time she pointed out my actions to my dad, who was right there for each of them. It was incredible to see just how she celebrated my accomplishments. I thought of slapping Jack for our own moment earlier with Aurora.

"I'm just so proud of our little genius; she learned all of that today," she said continuing to blow kisses to me with my dad. I would return them at random before letting out a little giggle and clapping excitedly. Mimicking the whole production my mom was performing. She was also, blowing a kiss, clapping her hands and giggling with me. This went on for several minutes before my dad slowed his momentum with the pattern.

"Did you guys get to have dinner already?" he asked looking down at the clock. "You know it's 7:00?" He told her pointing his watch face toward hers.

"Oh no. It's not. She demanded looking out the playroom door to the small clock that hung on the wall between our front windows. Sure enough it read after 7:00. "Oh honey, Mommy missed dinner she was so excited." She jumped up and scooped me up before bolting from the room. "You were just too impressive my little Emma Bemma, I didn't even know," she said half explaining to me, half defending herself to my dad.

When we turned into the kitchen, the room faded and I stood there at my bedside table staring at my now fully charged phone. I looked down at the small section of my pants that still had some of the bathwater from my earlier celebration. I let out a small chuckle to myself and went back to her room hearing a faint "threee, four, five" escape from the room into the hallway.

Chapter Twenty-One

Birthday Party

"**W**hat is this thing?" I shouted at the perforated cardboard pieces I had been fighting with for the past hour. I added my now ruined tenth attempt to the pile and reread the instructions, again. I growled getting to step four.

"Somehow there are only seven steps in this origami hell," I said to myself picking up another flat cardboard piece to start the process again "Yet somehow it is impossible."

I held the paper close to me and matched the perforated edges to the small image in step one. I started the first step for now the eleventh time, "Okay" I said to myself letting out a deep breath. I moved onto step two turning the paper to again match the small image in the instructions. I folded the two sides in since step three was a two-fer. I felt my skin crawl now that I was approaching step four. I started to pull the edges together as the image depicted for step four. I heard the cardboard squeak, resisting, the more I pulled them toward each other the less and less it looked like the picture from step four.

Rip... I heard the paper announce. I dropped the cardboard on our kitchen table and put my head in my hands.

"There is absolutely no way!" I shouted louder this time at the ripped cardboard laying in front of me. I tossed the ruined eleventh attempt to the pile and noticed Jack standing in the doorway.

"How was it going in here?" he said with caution standing safely in the dark hallway.

I looked down at the small graveyard of wood-patterned folded up cardboard pieces that were now garbage and rolled my eyes at Jack.

"The instructions make no sense, the folding doesn't work, I'm just burning through these stupid boxes" I felt the knot in my throat. I could still see the image in my head, the cute little box promised in step seven. The picture depicted the pre-cut cardboard with fold lines to be folded in a way to create small chest with a handle. At the end the box would look like a treasure chest and I planned to fill each with candy, fake jewelry, eye patches, and other knick knacks I picked up over the past two weeks.

"So it's not going? Do you want help?" he asked walking into the light of the kitchen and squinting, studying the pile in front of me and the instructions between us.

"Yes, call the crazy person at this stupid ass company and ask them how the hell step four would ever work with the cardboard in this stupid pack." I half shouted at him pushing the instructions in his direction, hoping this would be enough for him to fix it all for me.

"Okay but they are probably closed, do you know it's 1:00 a.m.?" he asked picking up the instructions that landed in front of him.

"But I still have to decorate the cupcakes, finish all of the goodie bags, decorate the table, and set the games up," I said feeling my body start to sweat.

This was her first big party. Her whole class was coming plus a few friends from her swimming class. I had the whole day mapped in my head at this point and wanted everything to match that image. My heart sped up when I went through my to-do list again. Realizing all I still had to get ready for the party.

"Let me fight with these things," he said sitting down next to me and picking up the next victim in the package "just relax and I'll take care of it."

"Good luck" I told him backing away from the table. "Just make sure we have thirty-one at the end of it" I pointed at the front of the second package that read 'twenty-four count'. "I've wasted eleven already."

"I got it." he replied starting to follow the instructions and making the first fold with care.

"I have to work on the ring-toss game." I explained pointing my thumb over my shoulder. Really I just needed space from my failure spread across the kitchen counter.

I went into the dining room to start pulling the other supplies I had purchased to decorate the house. Normally we are all set for every party at least days in advance. But this year her birthday fell on a Monday so we had a family dinner that night. Tuesdays are Girl Scout night and I wanted to be snack mom and let everyone celebrate her birthday there too. Wednesday we brought her up to see her friend that moved away, their birthdays were only three days apart. Thursday she wanted to make cupcakes to bring to her classroom for school on Friday. I was planning to take off Friday and work on things all day then we could assemble the house once she was asleep but as luck would have it she woke up with an ear infection Thursday night and we spent 2 hours at the doctor before spending another hour at the pharmacy. She still wanted to bring the cupcakes in to her classroom so we did that at the end of the day. So that wasted all of Friday and I didn't end up getting to start the whole party craziness until after she fell asleep at 9:00 o'clock tonight.

I picked up the tablecloth and saw the three hooks with the cardboard I had purchased to make "pirate ring toss" a simple idea I stumbled upon online. I grabbed the supplies: the black trifold cardboard, three hooks, paint, and hot glue gun. I started to set up this next project by the nearest outlet in the dining room. I contemplated joining Jack in the kitchen and felt the annoyance set in, I can't get anywhere near those stupid goodie boxes, even the thought of them stressed me out.

I plugged the hot glue gun into the outlet and balanced the gun on the small stand at the tip. I waited for the gun to heat up and evaluated the items on the table. Starting to stress about the remaining list in my head of all that we need done by tomorrow. I heard a faint grumble come from the other room; I restrained from checking in on Jack and returned to the project in front of me.

The glue gun began to leak melted glue I picked up the gun and fastened down the pirate emblem and three hooks to the board. After the hooks were on the board I picked up the bag of fake booty and started to glue the small gold plastic discs to the board at random. I started to get in the rhythm with this and felt less stressed about at least this project. I zoned out on the plastic golden coins filling the empty space on the board. The gun began to expel more and more glue with each coin. Strings of glue covered the table, cardboard, and me. This would inform anyone paying attention that the gun had reached a temperature much higher than needed to melt glue. I didn't notice the cues.

"Ouch" I yelped when a string of melted glue missed the coin and landed in the middle of my palm.

"You okay?" I heard him call from the other room.

"Yeah," I replied peeling the hardening glue from my reddened palm. "Damned glue gun..." I continued assessing the board and pulling the plug from the wall. *That'll have to work*, I thought. I put the gun down knowing for my own safety the project had to be done.

The bright light came and I was pulled from my throbbing hand, replaced in a kitchen standing with a filthy apron. It was still dark outside but I was no longer in my house. I was in my childhood home mixing a bowl of some kind of chocolate batter. To the right were three round baked cakes on individual cooling racks and a bowl of blue frosting.

"Just one more." I heard her say to my dad who stood on the other end of the counter shoving another handful of candy into a fish-shaped piñata.

"You said that on the last one." he said pointing toward the several circular cakes that sat between them. "You have been baking since yesterday." he said shaking the piñata so candy could fall deeper into the fish.

"But that wasn't cake." she said turning and pointing to the sugar cookies in the shape of fish and the rice Krispy treats that sat on the counter behind her.

"These parents are not going to appreciate you feeding their kids three desserts and sending them home with candy." he said shaking a handful of candy at her before he pushed it into the paper fish.

"Don't remind me. I still have to put all of that together," she said wiping her hands on the apron and glancing at the colorful bags all lined up next to toys and trinkets on the far end of the counter.

She dumped the batter into a circular baking pan and pushed the whole thing into the oven. I felt her turn back to the counter to pull together all the goodies. She opened each small bag of toys and games and assembled them in a line in front of her. I saw the small items and recalled the birthday. I don't remember how old I was, but this was such a fun birthday. My mom made this huge blue under the sea themed cake and we played this fishing game with a small child swimming pool.

I used to always laugh with my classmates after that party. When we were hitting the piñata, the third person to take their turn, Chris I think his name was, hit the fish square and the whole thing ripped from the rope it was hanging from. The fish ironically landed in the small swimming pool and was instantly destroyed. Some of the candy inside was ruined too, all the lollipops and smarties were violated by the water, but any sealed packages remained intact. The second that fish splashed into the pool all the kids scrambled to attain their candy when the contents fell out of the soaked paper fish. Mixed in with the candy were little colorful pieces of tissue paper from the piñata fish. The fish deteriorated into garbage mixing in with all of our candy. Even though almost half the candy was destroyed and kids collected handfuls of garbage with their attempts to grab the most candy, it was so funny at the time. I thought about this memory watching my mother assemble goodie bags. It was such a great time and the flying fish piñata was the talk of the class for weeks.

I let my memory fade and returned to my mother. Her body was almost robotic while she filled the bags, she would take one toy or candy from each of the piles in her line then tie the whole bag with a ribbon. When she tied up the bags, she added the finished goodie bags into a large basket. It was odd seeing all these items before they were used for my party.

I recognized the toys, the baggies, even the large basket we used for parties and Thanksgiving bread. It was like I was seeing the man behind the curtain in the Wizard of Oz. The magic was so real when I was little. The excitement for the day— the toys and games and all the sweets. The magic was so much more powerful now that I thought about the time I just left, my husband and I preparing the games and toys for the party. The stress of creating the perfect day for our daughter drove our efforts to excess.

I was pulled back from my memories by my mom's voice.

"Are you sure we shouldn't have one more game?" she asked my dad keeping her focus on the bags she was filling. "I'm just afraid the kids are not going to have fun."

"I think you have more than enough." he replied shaking the piñata again and continuing to push more candy into the hole in the top.

"I guess, at least it's supposed to be nice out so we can have them play outside after the piñata, fishing, and crafting. That should work if they start to get bored."

"It will be fine, you would think you were planning her wedding," he laughed "you have been buying supplies, coordinating all these activities, and building this piñata for the past few months. I still can't conceive how you managed to make this. In a thousand years I would never believe someone could just make a piñata." He adjusted the fish rolling his fingers over the feathery paper.

"What was I supposed to do, she specifically asked for a fish piñata and the store didn't have any." she replied looking at her creation. "Don't rip that thing, it needs to survive with the weight of all that candy until some kid smacks it out." she joked at him swinging a completed goodie bag at the frilly colorful fish.

I searched my memories, asked for a piñata? I had no memory of asking for this particular piñata but there it sat. And somehow she made it I thought watching my mom continue to put together goodie bags. I thought back to her look of horror when the piñata landed in the water. No wonder she stood there in shock when all the children attacked the water soaked candy and fish. I felt horrible thinking of how much time she must have spent, I don't even want to know the steps that go into making a piñata. Personally, I don't even know where that process would start. I thought of the yellow, orange, blue, and green tissue paper that disintegrated into the water.

Again, I was pulled back from my thoughts, my dad cleared his throat and said "So, um, should there be a timer going or something?" Pointing to the oven.

"What?" My mom shouted dropping the goodie bag she was working on and turning to face the oven. "I didn't realize, I must have forgot." she stammered throwing the door open and reaching in to grab the burnt smelling cake.

"Hon!" I heard my dad call to her. I watched her bare hand reach in and grab the cake pan.

"DAMMIT!" she screamed as she instinctively pulled her hand back throwing the burnt cake to the floor. "Damn, damn, damn." she followed up holding her hand close to her body and jumping around the kitchen.

My dad rushed around the counter to her and pulled her hand out to run under cold water at the sink.

"Are you okay?" he asked examining her hand under the cold water.

"Well I just burned a cake, then I burned me," she said rolling her hand under the cold water. "I can't believe I forgot a timer" she cried slumping over the sink.

My dad turned from her side and started to clean up the cake that sat on the floor under the upturned cake pan.

"So I guess it's going to be a three layer cake…" he started.

"It's not funny yet." she shot back turning to face him with her hand under the cold running water. "I just want her to have a good birthday. I don't want to let her down, she deserves a great birthday party. I need it to be perfect for her."

"You built her a piñata," he said pointing at the fish the lay on the counter. "I still don't know how you did that one." he laughed coming back to the sink to assess her hand.

"That's all she wanted for her party, I had to make it happen."

"How's your hand?" he asked examining the reddened area.

"I should be fine," she responded. "I still have to finish the cake."

My dad opened his mouth to object.

"Don't worry I will give up on this whole 4th layer thing, the oven is going off." she said using her non-burned hand to turn off the oven. "I have to decorate it," she smiled and motioned to the blue icing.

I felt myself return to my dining room. I could feel her burned hand still throbbing while I became aware of my surroundings again. It occurred to me it wasn't her burnt hand it was mine. I looked down at the red blotch on my palm and thought of the memory. I reached up to my neck and rubbed the bottom edge of the heart thinking about my mom.

I thought of my childhood memory of this great birthday and all the fun I had. I recalled the flying fish that splashed into the kiddie pool and my mom's shocked face watching in horror while her hard work become garbage.

At the time I had no idea of the effort that went into this colorful paper fish that didn't even survive three children with a bat. I felt a smile build on my face and my eyes began to well with tears. I stared at my ring toss project thinking of the memory I just experienced. I felt a tear break the ridge of my lashes and creep down my face then heard a squeak in the floor.

I looked up and Jack stood on the other side of the table staring down at me on the floor.

"You're right," he announced "Step four is impossible."

"Huh?" I asked wiping the tear rolling down my face and staring back at him.

"Those stupid boxes, there is no way you can fold the corners it shows in step 4 without ripping the thing to shreds."

"Oh, so how many did you ruin?" I asked getting up from table and standing up the ring toss game in its completed state.

"Let's just say all of them." he responded. "Sorry it became a game I would not let myself lose. Then I got to the end of the second package. I can run to the store in a few hours and get more or something else that works." he offered letting the defeat creep into his words.

"No," I replied. "I have an idea." I told him walking back into the kitchen. I opened the drawer and pulled out the box of baggies we have stockpiled for Aurora's snacks and lunches.

"We already have the goodies, here are the bags. Ta-da, goodie bags." I sang to him tossing the box next to the piles of toys and candies on the kitchen table.

"You seem less stressed" he said almost confused looking at the box of simple bags.

I just smiled at him picturing the three tiered cake and paper fish from my memory.

I crossed into the kitchen to start putting the goodie bags together with him. Using my non-burnt hand to collect the items and drop into the impromptu bags, I thought of my mom again. She did so much for me that day; I never really knew any of that. I felt so remorseful. *Did I thank her enough that year?* I thought of her desperation for the perfect party for little me. I thought of the weeks leading up to this day and the time I spent researching games, decoration ideas, and the several runs to party supply stores. I felt my body warm comparing the time we devoted to our daughters. I smiled and watched our hands continue to work on assembling the goodie bags.

I was shaken back to reality when Jack repeated his question,

"...is there?" He asked staring at my face.

"Is there what?" I asked looking up at him.

"Is there anything else we need to assemble?" he asked again.

"Just be glad we don't have to make a piñata," I said grinning at him.

"A piñata?" he asked "I don't think you can just make a piñata…"

"Oh trust me, you can," I said as I giggled a little, thinking again of this soaring fish that took a dive into the kiddie pool.

We continued to work on the goodie bags and I told him about my party.

"My mom made me a fish piñata once…" I said with a huge smile on my face.

Chapter Twenty-Two

Tell Me About Grandma

My mind was still swimming when we pulled the pillows from the bed later that night. I looked up at Jack lost with how to even bring up what had happened. Finally, he caught my eyes, I stuttered out "She asked, she asked about her grandma..." He looked confused and concerned. Why was this so hard for me, I waited for him to follow up and press me for more. Finally, he sat down on his side of the bed with his body aimed at me and asked, "What did you say?"

"I panicked, I told her she died when I was little and I barely knew her."

"That's all you said?"

I searched the floor feeling guilty now. "I told her it's late and she had to go to bed."

"Honey, you and me both know you have a special connection with your mom that you aren't able to fully explain, how could you tell her you barely knew her?"

I felt this comment stab me in the heart, I felt sick. He was right, I knew more about my mom than my father at this point. I grew up with her, learned from her life. I had a direct unfiltered view into her past, and she gave all that to me.

I looked down, I couldn't meet his eyes. There was a soft noise and he shifted on the bed closer to me.

"Why don't you tell her more when you're ready? I know you still miss your mom and it's going to be hard, but don't you want Aurora to know more about her?"

That familiar flash and back I went. I found myself sitting on a bed, a hospital bed? I looked around and it was more familiar. It wasn't a hospital bed; it was my mom's room. I could hear music from the movie 'The Little Mermaid' seeping in from outside the door. Then my mom turned to face my dad, he looked so young here. He wasn't yet aged from the pain of losing her. Even without those lines he still had that same sad quiet face, it always looked on the verge of tears.

"I don't know how to leave, I can't leave her Leo. How can she grow up without a mom, without me?"

He stared down swallowing hard. "You never know..." he started.

She interrupted him and waved her arms as if this was the 100th time he had started this sentence. "We need to be realistic here Leo, we know just as much as every doctor now. We see the numbers and the scans." She explained as if she had no emotional attachment to this information. "We can't just ignore it all. We know it is inevitable and getting closer every moment."

He sighed nodding his head with his eyes closed "Do you want to try to talk to her again?"

"She's too young I can't try to explain death and tell her what her life will be like after me. I can't tell her about safe sex and give her words of wisdom for her wedding day."

I felt the warm tears streaming down and her eyes closing. A cold splash hit her neck and I felt the necklace sitting there. I could feel the necklace get cold against her skin now soaked in her tear. She was thinking about my whole future while I watched yet another Disney movie no doubt while singing and dancing along right outside her door.

She opened her eyes and looked at my dad again, "I don't want to just leave her letters. I could never imagine reading letters from my mom from beyond the grave." She fought back more tears with a painful wince and attempted to move on the bed. "I just want her to be alright."

"She will be." My dad interrupted starting to wipe the tears and reassessing the pillows surrounding my mom.

She turned her head to the side where bright colored papers laid shuffled around in her bedside drawer. It was obvious that she was thumbing through them, she had several on her bed and the rest remained in the drawer. I realized these were the drawings I had made in her room. I never saw where they all went so I assumed they were thrown away after she took them. I watched her look over the pictures in her lap and hands; all these simple flowers, stick people, lopsided houses, round bright suns, and one horrible attempt at some four-legged creature, that was brown and took up most of the middle of the yellow paper. She turned her head back and I felt just how weak she was at this point. The room spun and she closed her eyes.

"I just want her to remember me and know I love her." She squeezed out with urgency in her words.

My dad tilted his head and then turned to face the door.

"I will tell her every day, I won't let her forget you."

236

Again she looked around the room, across from the bed next to a collection of prescription bottles and other medical supplies; there was a line of photos of me. Baby photos, zoomed in images of my face, smiling and silly faces. Not one photo contained her or my dad. Further to the right was a bunch of my toys piled around a chair that only I could fit in. Against the wall were boxes of crayons with tattered corners and a stack of coloring books.

I remember sitting in that corner, confused and afraid to look at my mom. I never knew what was going on when I was so little. I just knew that this room made me sad and my mom couldn't leave it. I would go in there just about every day and play or color while my mom just lay in her bed.

I was jolted back from thinking of my time in this room when she started to feverishly explain a plan to my dad. "I want to make a photo album for her; I'm going to need your help and Kayla. Can you get all my photos together and I'll tell Kayla to get some album supplies."

I remember Kayla from the few years after my mom had passed. She was a friend that she had from before I was born that would babysit and come over to see my mom a few times a month. After she was gone, Kayla used to try to help my dad and be a female influence in my life. She would take me out to do my nails or get my hair cut before bringing me home.

After a few years, Kayla had to move because of her job. She spent a few weeks around all the time until I didn't see her anymore. We still get holiday cards and she still calls to wish me happy birthday. But Kayla like many of my mom's old friends was pulled into her own life.

I felt another cold splash and a new tear fell from the twisted vines of the necklace onto her chest. She grabbed for the heart hanging around her neck. With that motion there was a rush of warmth and she began to speak.

"And this, I want her to have this. I will tell her why when I give her the photo album." She continued holding the necklace out pressing the heart between her fingers.

She started to remove the clasp, I felt the cold sweat on her neck and my father's warm hands reaching back to help her.

The two removed the necklace and put it on the table to the left of the bed. Looking at this table, I saw more photos of my smiling face, one dressed up for Halloween with this unrecognizable version of Ariel. I remembered that Halloween. We never had the chance to go shopping because my mom was rushed to the hospital and it uprooted our life for a whole week. I remember staying at Grandpa's house and Kayla's house during the day then waking up at home to my dad. Each morning he prepared me for another day under their care. The night of Halloween my mom had returned home so my grandpa drove me home to see her. At that point, all major stores were closed and I had no costume. I was so upset I didn't want to go to the Halloween party that night, I threw such a fit. As a last resort my dad, with the help of my mom's instructions, put together a purple shirt with green pants and pinned, rolled up newspapers to create some semblance of a fin. Sometime in my parents' attempt to pull this together my dad ran out to the closest store and somehow found a fish stuffed animal. In the photo on my mom's desk you can still see my dried tears on my cheeks in the makeshift costume with a huge smile on my face while I just about squeezed the stuffing out of that fish. I felt her gaze go to the door where I was just outside trying to say the lines of the movie with each of the characters.

She sighed and whispered "Photos that's how she can remember me. I'll put all my favorite memories and tell her my stories and our stories together. It will be like her way to get to know me even when I'm not here." When the last three words left her mouth, I felt her swallow tears back and smile through it all to my dad. He smiled through his pain back to her. "If she can't have me for the future, I want to give her my past." She finished. The tears ran from both eyes racing down her face to her chin.

My mom looked back at the necklace and I felt myself return to my bedroom. Again Jack was staring at me like he usually does when I get pulled to my mom's memories. This one was different; I could feel the tears start. I looked at him, and swallowed hard to push my emotions back just long enough. "I need to call my dad"

"It's like eleven. Will he even be up?"

I didn't even take this into consideration; I started to find his name in my phone then put the receiver to my ear. Again swallowing before he answered, I felt tears forming while I thought about my question.

He answered on the second ring, "Hey my little girl, everything okay?"

I felt his concern over the phone but just blurted out my question.

"What happened to mom's photo album to me?"

He paused, "What photo album?"

"The one she wanted to make me."

"How... How did you know about that?"

I didn't answer; I waited for him to answer my question.

"We didn't have a chance to make it, she wanted to start right away and that's when she discussed giving you that necklace…"

I felt my necklace heavy on my neck. Instinctively I reached for it and swallowed hard again.

"I had all the photos ready and Kayla came over with all the supplies." He paused and I heard him fighting tears now too.

I looked at Jack for the first time since I dialed, he just sat staring at me. He studied my face while I held the phone with one hand and the necklace with the other. I rocked back and forth swaying my weight. It was a light enough fidget that I didn't look insane but I know I was concerning him.

"She passed that next day. We never did the photo album."

"What?" I blurted feeling my weight drop into my feet and my body stop rocking.

"I'm sorry sweetie, I didn't know you even knew about the album. She wanted so bad to make something for you so you always knew how much she loved you. So that you couldn't forget her. She told me to give you the necklace with the photo album. When she passed I didn't know what to do, so I gave you the necklace as she wanted."

I felt my thumb roll up and down the heart hanging on my neck and breathed out loud into the phone. I realized I've made it to the end, this is the last memory. If this was the last day she was here I've reached the end of my mom's memories and now won't get to see her. I felt my next breath come in staggered echoing through the phone to my dad.

"Are you okay? What even made you think about this?"

"Aurora asked about mom tonight."

"Oh," he let escape from his lips before rustling came through the phone. "I still have all the photos that she wanted to use if you want…"

"What?" I interrupted.

"I had everything ready for her to start when she passed, I didn't have the heart to put it all back and I couldn't make the album without her. I just couldn't, I kept it all boxed up," he continued to explain letting his voice trail off. "I didn't know what to do after…"

"Yes, yes I want it." I blurted out looking to Jack again.

"Okay, I can stop by tomorrow morning. Get some sleep sweetie."

He had to get off the phone I heard him fighting with each breath to not cry with me on the line. There was only so much he could handle when it came to reminiscing about her.

I let him hang up and looked back to Jack who couldn't wait any longer.

"Photo album? Was it your mom's?" he asked.

I realized now, that although she never had a chance to give me the photo album, her necklace let me see her past, just like she wanted. I felt an urge of appreciation for this small silver token that's been hanging on my neck bringing me my mom.

I responded, "She was going to make me one but she passed before she had the chance to start." I dropped my hand from my necklace. "She also gave me the necklace and was going to tell me why later."

He wrapped his arms around me hugging for a long moment before pulling away to look at my face.

"So do you know why she gave you the necklace?" he asked while he studied my teary face.

Past his inquiring face I could see photos of our daughter, artwork of unrecognizable animals and stick figure people, and the toys piled up where we played earlier that day in the corner of the room by the closed toy bin.

"To give me all of her she could..." I answered automatically. I was thinking of all her past that she was able to share with me.

CഅChapter Twenty-Threeℭᐧᕽᕽᕽᕽᕽᕽ

SHARING GRANDMA

The next morning I woke up early, I had some kind of mission in my head forming. I wasn't sure what I was thinking just yet. Everything from last night was still swimming in my mind. I went into my daughter's room and told her that Grandpa was coming over and she was going to see photos of Grandma. She jumped from her bed and shouted "Let's make him pancakes." zipping past me out of the room.

Now that the whole house smelled of the starchy cakes and of course bacon, we sat down and forced my dad to stay for breakfast. He had tears echoing in his eyes from either last night or this morning and avoided the box he brought with its painful contents. Once he placed it on the counter, he gave the box a wide berth and avoided even looking in its direction. Aurora was too excited and proud of her pancakes that she had already forgotten the whole reason for his visit. Luckily she didn't bring up the box that we hadn't touched since his arrival. Aurora rattled off the whole meal to my dad. He stole glances at me, studying to see when I would approach the box.

I started to think back to that memory of my mom, somehow she must have known that the necklace would share her with me. Again I felt my thumb on that familiar point on the bottom of the heart.

My father watched me get lost in my own mind, "Aurora do you want to show me your new trick on the swings?" he asked.

Most of breakfast she was spouting about two things, her amazing pancake skills and her ability to hang from her hands on the highest bar in her swing set. He met my eyes and the two of them went out to the backyard. As he closed the screen door behind him he whispered, "They are all in that purple box there on the counter," even though we all knew exactly where the photographs were.

Sitting on the counter was a faded box with a fine layer of dust sitting on the top, you could tell that he had wiped most of the dust away but this layer was so embedded it was now part of the cardboard itself. I saw the box and had a distant memory of seeing this object in the corner of her room the day my dad cleaned it out. With that thought my body froze, I couldn't physically move.

Jack took my staring to be an invitation for help; he picked up the box and put it between us. He waited for me to lift the lid. I just moved my breakfast plate to the side and continued to stare down willing him to help me while my body sat paralyzed. I listened to the rustling plastic when he picked up the first item on the box. He looked in the bag, "It looks like this was going to be the album," he said pointing the opening at me and I saw the scrapbook supplies, pens, stickers, papers, and a hard white book with a simple pink heart on the cover. He pulled out items and spread them on the table the receipt fell and bounced in front of me. There it was, the date printed on the top of the receipt right above the cashier's name was the day before my mom died. The time on the paper was late so Kayla must have run the errand and dropped off the supplies that night. I felt the tears running down now. I still couldn't get myself to peek at the box. I just felt the receipt between my fingers and wouldn't allow myself to break eye contact with the small slip of paper.

"Are you ready?" I heard Jack ask and move his chair closer.

"I think so." I tentatively whispered back hearing the scrape of cardboard from the lid against the bottom of the box.

He grabbed a pile of photographs from the box and began placing them in front of me. He placed each picture like he was dealing cards and building suspense with each one he put down. The first picture he put in front of me was our first picture together. I saw my small baby face peeking out under a hat and above a blanket, my exhausted mom smiled with pride holding me close. I remember this day, I went back in my mind and felt her pose for this picture at the hospital after I was born. With that I felt my tears slow. I already shared this with my mom and I was so happy for that.

With that feeling of appreciation, I turned and lifted my head so I could see all the other photos he laid out so far.

I saw her prom photo, with that familiar dress and my dad as her date. I remembered that night and her bravery. Hiding under that photo I saw her with her friend at summer camp, another memory she shared with me. I could remember her enjoyment and her friend Beth who remained in her life from summer camp up to the end. Jack removed more photos. There was an overexposed photo of the flash reflecting off glass with two young faces waving from the driveway.

I felt myself jump up and my tears returned. Different tears, happy tears. I was seeing all the memories with my mom again. I saw her holding her stomach and a small white and blue stick with my father behind her, the moment they found out about me. Then I saw my birthday party, my dad and mom standing behind me with the still intact fish piñata hanging behind us. I thought back to her making the fish and burning her hand on the cake. My eyes were then pulled to a banner at the top of the next photo that read 'HAPPY BIRTHDAY ROSIE!' with a small rose painted after the exclamation point. I followed the photo down and saw three smiling faces. My grandma, my grandpa and a squished version of my mother in between.

"This is when she got the necklace," I explained to Jack and myself. I reached up and rubbed the heart again.

I looked at Jack, he stayed seated next to me watching me wipe tears and smile. "That's why she gave me the necklace; she already shared all this with me."

I knew this confused him but he just smiled, "Maybe you should make the album" he suggested watching me thumb through more photos.

I half laughed, half cried in a blurt of sound that brought me back. "Yeah. Yeah, *I* can make it."

I heard the slider open and my dad stood there, "She wants to show you something." The two of us stared up at him. "Are you okay?" he followed studying the scene at our kitchen table.

I know my dad has always avoided conversations about my mom; it's too hard for him. I wiped my tears and grabbed a tissue. "Yes everything is fine." I replied with the growing smile on my face.

While we walked toward the door I heard "Mommy, Daddy, watch this." echoing through our yard.

We turned to see her hanging from the swing on her belly and spinning around with her hair falling toward the floor. The three of us stood there and clapped for her.

I turned to my dad "I'm going to make it for her."

He met my eyes and breathed out "I think she would like that." Then he turned toward Aurora so I could only see his face in profile. I could still see the tears start to swell in his eye. He must have felt me watching him so he moved toward the swings to escape. "I told you they would love it, let's see it again," he shouted to Aurora while he cleared the lump in his throat.

I turned back to Jack, "I'll share the photos with her." before I turned to watch my little girl spinning and laughing on the swings.

৫৴Chapter Twenty-Four৫৹

ROSE'S ALBUM

I finished the album that week, put all the photos in order and wrote to the best of my memories from my mom a description for each picture and event. The night I finished the book I was about to tuck Aurora in before I paused, "Aurora I have a new book for you."

"But I wanted Miss Piggy goes to the doctor," she announced.

"How 'bout we do that twice tomorrow, this book is very special."

She started to return her book to the shelf and informed me "Three times tomorrow," working her way into the middle of her bed and waiting for me to pull the blankets up to her belly button.

I pulled out the white album with a simple pink heart, in the middle. I had inscribed Rose to the best of self-taught calligraphy skills.

"This is your middle name." I explained.

"Rose?" she sounded out each letter forming the name.

"Yes, and you have that name from my mother."

"Is this her book?" she asked looking up at me.

248

"Yes." I told her.

I opened the front cover and smiled. Now our daughter will know about her too. I flipped through the pages and my smile grew with each turn while I told her about her grandma. Each page made me more aware of the necklace and the memories I had seen over the years. I read each blurb under the photograph adding the emotions I had felt during each visit with the memory. I was so happy that it wasn't just a book of photographs, it was a book of my mother. I had looked through these eyes at each photo being captured and felt the smile on her face, tears dried to her cheeks, and love in her heart. I felt myself slow on certain photos taking time to swallow the lump that had rushed to my throat. Aurora waited for me each time and just examined the glossy photograph until I was ready to start talking again.

We arrived at the last photo in the book a simple picture of my mother smiling. This was one of the last photos we had before she got sick, she still had her full cheeks and bright eyes. It used to be resting in my dad's bedroom but he brought it over one afternoon instructing me to add it to the book. I thought it was perfect. For years that was my favorite picture because it was so simple and sweet. I know he had always loved this picture too. It was from a time before his whole world was ripped from beneath him. Even with that, he gave me the photograph for the album to Aurora with one simple last thought, "Thanks for finishing her album, sweetie." The two of us hugged and quiet tears fell down our cheeks. No more was needed to be said. I brushed her face at the end of the book and listened to Aurora gleam about my mother and the pictures we just saw.

At the end I closed the white album and Aurora looked up and asked "Do you miss grandma?"

"Sometimes, but I know she's always with me." I replied with a light sniffle.

"How?" She asked.

"She shared these memories with me and I know she will always love me."

"And now you're sharing them with me?" she asked hugging the book.

"Yes"

"She was really pretty." She commented tilting her head.

I looked down at her and said "Yes, just like you," brushing her hair back.

I took the album and lay it on her bedside table before reaching back to remove my necklace. The necklace that my mom gave to me with her memories attached. I felt myself pause on the clasp, and closed my eyes, I opened the delicate silver and removed the necklace for the first time in years.

"She would want you to have this too, she gave this to me when I was little so I could remember every day just how much she loved me." I explained trying to form a smile even though my face rebelled from me.

"Does she love me too?" she asked looking up at me.

"Of course she does."

I explained to her that she would have to wait like I did to wear it. The necklace was very precious and she was too little to wear it just yet. I hung the silver heart from a picture frame on her dresser. Then I made room for the album on her bookshelf next to pictures of our last family vacation to the beach and her sitting with her grandfather in our old house. I tucked Aurora in and saw that familiar beat-up fish from

Halloween stained and missing half of one eye between her pillow and the wall. I smiled to myself and hit the light, "Good night my little peanut." When I shut the door I could see the hallway light reflecting off the heart, thanking me for telling her story.

Epilogue

Five Years Later

The door swung open and I heard the jingling of zippers when Aurora came crashing in with her backpack from summer camp. I heard Jack fighting in the garage with her the rest of her bags.

"How was it?" I shouted running to her. I could see the heart necklace hanging from her neck over her tie-dyed shirt and tangled with her handmade necklace from camp.

"It was so much fun, can I go again next year? Ashley is going to try to go too."

"Ashley was your friend you told me about in the letters?" I clarified when we peeled away from our long overdue hug.

"Yeah." She came around the counter with me to sit on the couch in the living room.

"So tell me about it." I implored.

I weighed her pause while I started to pull items from the bag to start on laundry. Dropping each item in the basked to bring to our washer. Her deliberate pause had stretched on for a few handfuls of clothes, I turned to see what had pulled her attention.

She was running her finger across a frame containing the picture of our wedding that stood on the table beside her. I watched her bring the photo close to her face and examine it. I sat waiting for her to tell me about her past few weeks even though we had talked by letters every other day.

"Do you think Ashley can be in my wedding too?" She asked as if she had waited long enough to get this out.

"I supposed so, why?" I replied holding my breath.

"Just like grandma's friend Beth..."

I thought back to the photo album with the descriptions I had added for Aurora that announced Beth in the summer camp photo with the added detail that Beth was also one of my mom's bridesmaids. She must have remembered that note from the album.

I was getting ready to respond to her when she returned the frame and added "And like your friend Brittney."

I looked up from her bag, "How did you know I met Brittney at camp." I searched through my memories. Did I ever tell her? I never left it out but I don't think I ever specifically told her she was from that same camp too. We knew each other for many years so I never accounted for how we first met when talking to my daughter about her.

She squinted her eyes and pondered how to start. "I'm not sure how to explain it, I saw grandma at summer camp and then I saw you at summer camp. I recognized Brittney from this photo of you and Daddy's wedding day." she pointed at the photo over her shoulder.

"You saw?"

"Yeah kind of like a flash then a dream I couldn't get out of." She searched her mind to explain. "But I didn't really see you or grandma. I was you and grandma."

I started to cry pulling her in for a hug.

"You saw?" I asked without needing an answer. I didn't know how much I had hoped for this to happen until right now. I felt relief rush over me while my confused little girl waited for more information.

I sighed through my tears before untangling the silver heart from the homemade necklaces she had added over the past few weeks.

"This was grandma's necklace remember, she gave it to me and I gave it to you." I explained.

She stared at me, and I let out a deep breath rubbing the bottom of the necklace I had worn for so long. It was odd how much I missed this familiar edge between fingers.

"They are memories from grandma, from her necklace."

She put her hands in between mine to reach the necklace, questioning me. "You saw them too?"

"Yeah that's how I got to know your grandma after she passed." I explained, my voice faltering. I was so elated to learn the silver heart gave the same gift to my daughter. I had not intended to hold this in the back of my mind, but there it sat. Now that I knew she saw them too my heart was singing loud in my chest. I was thanking my mother for the gift she gave to us both.

"How? How does it work?" She asked pressing the precious silver heart between her fingers.

"Love is what makes it work." I paused remembering all the memories my mother shared with me and now her. I smiled brighter thinking of all the things she would get to see and know from both of us.

"There will be more." I kissed her on the forehead and hugged her while she sat holding the necklace with one hand. I felt her squeeze tighter into the embrace. We were both so excited for the memories to come.

About the Author

April Waverly grew up in Connecticut working as an accountant while always exploring creative outlets. Through the years she would doodle tattoos, whip up unique cupcakes and even try her hand at painting from nail art to canvases. April loved to discover new means to explore her creativity. It has always been something that kept her in balance, numbers at work that were black and white and creative escapes providing a splash of color.

During her pregnancy with her first daughter a conversation with her mother inspired a story. After the idea was sparked she sat and wrote her first book 'One Shared Heart'. Through moments with her growing daughter and memories of her own she continued to find inspiration for the story. Since completing that first book, ideas continue to find her and demand that she share their stories as well.